Airbnb Mortgage Loans with No Income Verification

How to Get Approved Without Tax Returns Using DSCR and Alternative Documentation

By Joseph G. Correa

Licensed Mortgage Broker, Finibi Mortgage

Copyright & Legal Notice

Published by Live Stronger Faster

The information provided in this book is for educational and informational purposes only and should not be construed as financial, legal, or tax advice. Readers are encouraged to consult with licensed professionals before making any financial or real estate decisions. The author and publisher assume no responsibility for any losses or damages incurred as a result of the use or misuse of the information contained in this publication.

First Edition, 2026

Table of Contents

Foreword

The world of mortgage lending is evolving faster than ever before, and nowhere is this more evident than in the rise of no-income verification loan strategies for short-term rental investors. As traditional lending continues to rely heavily on tax returns, W-2 income, and strict debt-to-income ratios, a growing number of entrepreneurs, self-employed individuals, and real estate investors are finding themselves locked out of opportunities—not because they lack financial strength, but because their income does not fit inside outdated underwriting models. This is where Airbnb mortgage loans with no income verification step in, creating a powerful bridge between real-world cash flow and lender qualification. This book is designed to show you exactly how that bridge works, how to cross it successfully, and how to use it to scale your portfolio faster than most investors ever thought possible.

If you are self-employed, run multiple businesses, write off significant expenses, or simply prefer not to disclose traditional income, you are not alone. In fact, many of the most successful real estate investors operate outside the rigid structures that banks prefer. The challenge has never been a lack of income—it has been proving that income in a way that satisfies conventional underwriting guidelines. This is the fundamental shift you must understand: no-income verification does not mean no qualification. It means qualifying differently. Instead of focusing on what you report on paper, lenders begin to evaluate what your properties actually produce. This shift from personal income to property performance is what unlocks the true potential of Airbnb investing.

At the core of this transformation is the rise of DSCR loans—Debt Service Coverage Ratio financing—which allows borrowers to qualify based on the income generated by the property itself rather than their personal tax returns. But DSCR is only one part of the equation. Bank statement loans, asset-based strategies, and hybrid documentation methods all play a role in creating flexible approval pathways. Each option comes with its own advantages, requirements, and strategic use cases. The purpose of this book is to break down these options in a way that is clear, practical, and immediately applicable, so you can choose the right structure for your specific situation and goals.

Understanding the difference between bank statement loans, DSCR loans, and true no-doc strategies is critical if you want to succeed in this space. Bank statement loans analyze deposits over time to estimate income, making them ideal for business owners with consistent cash flow but complex tax returns. DSCR loans focus on rental income, making them powerful for Airbnb properties with strong occupancy and pricing strategies. True no-doc loans, while more rare and often requiring stronger credit or reserves, eliminate traditional income documentation altogether and rely heavily on overall borrower strength. Each of these paths is not just a loan product—it is a strategic tool, and learning how to use these tools effectively is what separates average investors from those who scale rapidly.

One of the most important concepts you will learn in this book is that lenders are not simply approving or denying loans—they are evaluating risk. When you remove traditional income documentation from the equation, other factors become more important. Credit score becomes a stronger indicator of reliability. Liquidity and reserves demonstrate your ability to handle unexpected challenges. Property performance metrics show whether the investment can sustain itself. This means that your success in securing no-income verification loans is not random—it is something you can engineer. By positioning your credit, structuring your reserves, and selecting the right properties, you can dramatically increase your approval odds and secure better loan terms.

For Airbnb investors, this creates a unique advantage. Unlike long-term rental properties, short-term rentals have the potential to generate significantly higher income when managed correctly. This increased income potential can translate directly into stronger DSCR ratios, making properties easier to finance without relying on personal income. However, this also introduces complexity. Income can fluctuate based on seasonality, location, competition, and management quality. Lenders understand this, which is why appraisal methods, rental data sources, and conservative underwriting adjustments play a critical role in the approval process. Learning how to navigate these variables—and even use them to your advantage—is a key focus of this book.

Another major theme you will explore is the mindset shift required to operate in this space. Traditional borrowers think in terms of qualifying for a loan. Strategic investors think in terms of structuring a deal. When you approach Airbnb mortgage loans with no income verification, you are no longer just submitting an application—you are building a case. You are presenting a complete financial picture that demonstrates stability, opportunity, and calculated risk. This includes how you title the property, how you manage your accounts, how you document your reserves, and even how you present your rental projections. Every detail contributes to the overall narrative that lenders evaluate.

Self-employed borrowers, in particular, will find tremendous value in the strategies outlined in this book. Many entrepreneurs unknowingly limit their borrowing power by focusing solely on minimizing taxable income. While this can be beneficial from a tax perspective, it often creates challenges when applying for traditional loans. No-income verification strategies offer a way to bypass this limitation, but they still require careful planning. Understanding how to balance tax strategy with lending strategy is essential if you want to grow your real estate portfolio efficiently. This book will help you align those two worlds so they work together instead of against each other.

Credit positioning is another critical pillar of success in no-income verification lending. While these loans offer flexibility in documentation, they often require stronger credit profiles to offset perceived risk. This does not mean you need perfect credit, but it does mean that strategic improvements can have a significant impact on your loan options. Small changes—such as reducing utilization, timing applications correctly, and maintaining consistent payment history—can lead to better rates, lower down payments, and more favorable terms. Throughout this book, you will learn how to view your credit not just as a score, but as a tool that can be optimized for maximum leverage.

Equally important is the concept of reserves and liquidity. In the absence of traditional income documentation, lenders look closely at how much capital you have available after closing. Reserves provide a safety net that reassures lenders you can continue making payments even during periods of lower occupancy or unexpected expenses. For Airbnb investors, this is especially important due to the variability of short-term rental income. Building and presenting strong reserves is not just about meeting minimum requirements—it is about strengthening your entire loan profile and positioning yourself as a low-risk borrower.

As you progress through this book, you will begin to see that no-income verification lending is not a shortcut—it is a different path. It requires a deeper understanding of how lenders think, how properties are evaluated, and how deals are structured. But for those who master it, the rewards are significant. You gain the ability to acquire properties faster, scale without traditional income limitations, and operate with a level of flexibility that most investors never achieve. This is particularly powerful in the Airbnb space, where speed, adaptability, and creative financing often determine who wins and who gets left behind.

This book is not just about getting approved for a loan—it is about building a system. A system that allows you to identify the right opportunities, structure them effectively, and repeat the process over and over again. Whether your goal is to acquire your first Airbnb property without using tax returns, or to expand an existing portfolio using advanced financing strategies, the principles you will learn here are designed to support long-term growth. Every concept, every strategy, and every example is intended to move you closer to that goal.

By the time you complete this book, you will have a clear understanding of how to navigate bank statement loans, DSCR loans, and no-doc options. You will know how to position yourself as a strong borrower, how to select properties that meet lender criteria, and how to structure deals that align with your financial goals. More importantly, you will develop the confidence to operate outside traditional limitations and take control of your investing strategy. This is where real growth begins—not when you follow the rules everyone else is using, but when you understand the system well enough to use it differently.

The opportunity in front of you is significant. The demand for short-term rentals continues to grow, and the financing options available to investors are becoming more flexible and innovative. Those who understand how to leverage no-income verification strategies will be in a position to capitalize on this trend in a way that few others can. This book is your guide to doing exactly that—step by step, strategy by strategy, deal by deal. Welcome to the next level of Airbnb investing, where income is no longer a limitation, and your ability to structure deals becomes your greatest asset.

Chapter 1

Understanding No-Income Verification Airbnb Mortgage Loans

The foundation of no-income verification Airbnb mortgage lending begins with a simple but powerful concept: lenders are no longer primarily concerned with how much you earn personally, but rather how well the property you are purchasing or refinancing can perform financially. This shift represents one of the most important evolutions in modern real estate financing. For decades, borrowers were evaluated based on W-2 income, tax returns, and rigid debt-to-income ratios that often failed to reflect the true financial strength of entrepreneurs and investors. Today, with the growth of short-term rental platforms and alternative lending models, a new framework has emerged—one that prioritizes asset performance, liquidity, and borrower positioning over traditional income documentation.

To fully understand this concept, you must first recognize why traditional income verification creates limitations. Many real estate investors intentionally reduce their taxable income through deductions, write-offs, and strategic accounting. While this reduces tax liability, it also lowers the income that lenders can use to qualify the borrower. As a result, highly successful individuals often appear "unqualified" on paper despite having strong cash flow and significant assets. No-income verification loans solve this problem by shifting the focus away from tax returns and toward more relevant indicators of financial stability.

In the Airbnb investment space, this shift is especially powerful. Short-term rentals operate differently from long-term rentals, often generating higher income through nightly rates rather than fixed monthly leases. This creates a dynamic income profile that traditional underwriting struggles to evaluate. No-income verification loan programs, particularly DSCR loans, are designed to accommodate this variability by focusing on projected or actual rental income rather than personal earnings. This means that if a property can demonstrate strong income potential relative to its expenses, it can qualify for financing even if the borrower's personal income is minimal or difficult to document.

One of the key pillars of no-income verification lending is the Debt Service Coverage Ratio, commonly referred to as DSCR. This metric compares the property's income to its debt obligations, providing a clear picture of whether the property can sustain itself financially. A DSCR of 1.0 means the property generates exactly enough income to cover its mortgage payment. A DSCR above 1.0 indicates positive cash flow, while a DSCR below 1.0 suggests that the property may require supplemental income or reserves. In Airbnb lending, many lenders look for DSCR ratios between 1.0 and 1.25, although some programs allow for lower ratios depending on other compensating factors.

However, DSCR is only one component of the broader no-income verification landscape. Bank statement loans offer another pathway for borrowers who have consistent deposits but complex financial structures. Instead of analyzing tax returns, lenders review 12 to 24 months of bank statements to calculate an average monthly income. This approach is particularly useful for business owners who may not show high taxable income but maintain strong cash flow. In the context of Airbnb investing, bank statement loans can be used when DSCR alone is not sufficient or when the borrower wants to leverage personal or business income alongside property performance.

True no-documentation loans represent the most flexible—and often most misunderstood—category within this space. These loans require little to no income verification and instead rely heavily on credit, assets, and overall borrower strength. While they offer maximum flexibility, they also come with stricter requirements in other areas, such as higher credit scores, larger down payments, and significant reserves. For experienced investors with strong financial profiles, these loans can be a powerful tool for rapid portfolio expansion.

Another critical factor in no-income verification lending is property evaluation. Unlike traditional loans, where the borrower's income plays the central role, these loans place significant emphasis on the property's ability to generate revenue. For Airbnb properties, this often involves analyzing short-term rental data from sources such as Airbnb performance reports, market analytics tools, and comparable rental data. Appraisers may use specialized methods, including short-term rental income analysis, to estimate the property's earning potential. Understanding how these evaluations work—and how to select properties that perform well under these criteria—is essential for success.

Credit plays a more prominent role in no-income verification loans than many borrowers expect. Since lenders are not relying on traditional income documentation, they use credit history as a key indicator of financial responsibility. A strong credit profile can offset other perceived risks and lead to better loan terms, including lower interest rates and higher leverage. Conversely, weaker credit may limit options or require additional compensating factors such as higher reserves or lower loan-to-value ratios. This makes credit optimization a critical part of your overall strategy.

Liquidity and reserves are equally important. Lenders want to ensure that borrowers have sufficient funds to cover mortgage payments, maintenance, and unexpected expenses, especially given the variable nature of short-term rental income. Reserves are typically measured in months of mortgage payments and may range from three to twelve months or more, depending on the loan program and borrower profile. Building and maintaining strong reserves not only improves approval chances but also provides a financial cushion that supports long-term success.

It is also important to understand the role of loan-to-value (LTV) ratios in no-income verification lending. Because these loans carry a different risk profile, lenders often require larger down payments compared to traditional loans. LTV ratios may range from 70% to 80% for many DSCR and no-doc programs, although this can vary based on credit, property type, and overall borrower strength. A lower LTV reduces risk for the lender and increases the likelihood of approval, making it a key consideration when structuring your deal.

As you begin to connect these concepts, a clear picture starts to emerge. No-income verification Airbnb mortgage loans are not about avoiding requirements—they are about meeting a different set of requirements. Instead of proving income through tax returns, you are proving strength through property performance, credit, liquidity, and strategic structuring. This requires a more sophisticated approach, but it also opens the door to opportunities that traditional financing simply cannot provide.

The most successful investors in this space understand that every deal must be approached strategically. They analyze properties not just for potential appreciation, but for their ability to meet DSCR thresholds. They structure their finances to maximize credit and reserves. They choose loan programs that align with their long-term goals. This level of intentionality is what allows them to scale quickly and efficiently, often acquiring multiple properties in a relatively short period of time.

Ultimately, no-income verification lending represents a shift in control. Instead of being limited by how your income appears on paper, you gain the ability to leverage your knowledge, strategy, and resources to qualify for financing. This is particularly powerful in the Airbnb market, where income potential is often higher and more flexible than traditional rental models. By mastering the principles outlined in this chapter, you are laying the groundwork for a new approach to investing—one that prioritizes performance, flexibility, and growth.

Real-Life Math Example: Structuring a No-Income Verification Airbnb Deal

Imagine an investor named Sarah who wants to purchase an Airbnb property in a high-demand vacation market. The purchase price of the property is $500,000. Sarah is self-employed and writes off a significant portion of her income, making it difficult for her to qualify using traditional methods. Instead, she decides to pursue a DSCR loan.

The lender requires a minimum DSCR of 1.20 and allows up to 75% loan-to-value. This means Sarah must put down 25%, or $125,000, leaving a loan amount of $375,000. The interest rate on the loan is 7.5%, and the monthly principal and interest payment is approximately $2,620. When adding taxes and insurance, the total monthly housing expense comes to $3,100.

To qualify for the loan, the property must generate enough income to meet the DSCR requirement. This means the monthly rental income must be at least 1.20 times the monthly housing expense. In this case, $3,100 multiplied by 1.20 equals $3,720. This is the minimum monthly income required for the property to qualify.

Sarah analyzes Airbnb data for comparable properties in the area. She finds that similar homes generate an average daily rate of $220 and maintain an average occupancy rate of 70%. To calculate monthly income, she multiplies $220 by 30 days, resulting in $6,600 in potential monthly revenue at full occupancy. She then applies the 70% occupancy rate, which brings the projected monthly income to $4,620.

With a projected income of $4,620 and a required income of $3,720, the property achieves a DSCR of approximately 1.49. This exceeds the lender's minimum requirement, making the deal eligible for financing. Importantly, Sarah did not need to provide tax returns or verify personal income to qualify—her approval was based entirely on the property's performance.

Next, Sarah considers reserves. The lender requires six months of reserves, which means she must have at least six months of the total housing expense available after closing. At $3,100 per month, this equals $18,600. Sarah ensures she has sufficient funds in her accounts to meet this requirement, further strengthening her loan profile.

She also reviews her credit score, which is 720. This places her in a favorable position, allowing her to secure competitive loan terms. If her credit score were lower, she might face a higher interest rate or stricter requirements, demonstrating the importance of credit positioning in no-income verification lending. After closing on the property, Sarah focuses on optimizing its performance. She invests in professional photography, dynamic pricing tools, and high-quality furnishings to maximize occupancy and nightly rates. Over time, she increases her average daily rate to $240 and improves occupancy to 75%, raising her monthly income to approximately $5,400.

This increased income not only improves her cash flow but also positions her for future opportunities. With a stronger performance history, she may be able to refinance the property, pull out equity, and reinvest in additional Airbnb properties. This is how investors use no-income verification loans not just to acquire properties, but to build scalable systems for growth.

Through this example, you can see how the numbers come together to form a complete picture. The key is not just understanding the formulas, but knowing how to apply them strategically. By selecting the right property, structuring the deal correctly, and positioning yourself as a strong borrower, you can leverage no-income verification loans to achieve your investing goals—regardless of how your income appears on paper.

Chapter 2

DSCR vs Bank Statement vs No-Doc Loans for Airbnb Investors

As you move deeper into the world of Airbnb mortgage financing without traditional income verification, one of the most important skills you can develop is the ability to choose the right loan strategy for each deal. Not all no-income verification loans are created equal, and understanding the differences between DSCR loans, bank statement loans, and true no-documentation loans will determine how efficiently you scale your portfolio. Each loan type is designed for a specific borrower profile and investment scenario, and the investors who grow the fastest are those who know exactly which tool to use at the right time.

At a high level, these three loan types represent different ways of answering the same question: how does the lender assess your ability to repay the loan without relying on traditional tax returns? DSCR loans answer that question by focusing on the property's income. Bank statement loans answer it by analyzing your cash flow through deposits. No-doc loans answer it by evaluating your overall financial strength, including credit, assets, and reserves. Each method removes reliance on tax returns, but replaces it with a different lens of risk evaluation.

DSCR loans are often considered the most powerful and scalable option for Airbnb investors. These loans are designed specifically for investment properties and are based almost entirely on the income generated by the property itself. Instead of calculating your personal debt-to-income ratio, lenders calculate the property's debt service coverage ratio by comparing its rental income to its total monthly expenses. This makes DSCR loans ideal for investors who want to separate their personal finances from their real estate investments and focus on building a portfolio driven by property performance.

For Airbnb properties, DSCR loans become even more attractive because of the higher income potential associated with short-term rentals. Unlike long-term leases, which are fixed and predictable, Airbnb income can be optimized through pricing strategies, seasonal adjustments, and improved property management. This creates opportunities to exceed DSCR requirements and unlock financing that would not be possible under traditional underwriting. However, this also introduces variability, and lenders often account for this by using conservative income estimates or requiring higher reserves.

Bank statement loans offer a different approach. Instead of focusing on the property alone, these loans evaluate your personal or business cash flow by reviewing deposits over a 12- or 24-month period. The lender calculates an average monthly income based on these deposits, often applying an expense factor to estimate net income. This approach is particularly useful for self-employed borrowers who have strong revenue but show low taxable income due to deductions. In the Airbnb context, bank statement loans can be used when the property's DSCR is not strong enough on its own, or when the borrower wants to leverage their broader financial activity.

One of the advantages of bank statement loans is flexibility. They allow borrowers to combine income sources, including multiple businesses, rental properties, and other revenue streams. This can create a stronger overall financial profile and increase borrowing capacity. However, this flexibility comes with additional documentation requirements compared to DSCR loans, and the approval process may be more complex. Investors must weigh these factors carefully when deciding which strategy to use.

True no-documentation loans represent the most flexible—but also the most selective—option in this category. These loans require little to no income verification and instead rely heavily on credit score, liquidity, and overall borrower strength. They are designed for high-net-worth individuals or experienced investors who can demonstrate financial stability through assets rather than income. While they offer maximum privacy and simplicity in terms of documentation, they often require larger down payments, higher reserves, and stronger credit profiles.

For Airbnb investors, no-doc loans can be particularly useful in situations where speed and simplicity are critical. For example, if you are competing for a high-demand property or need to close quickly, a no-doc loan may provide a faster path to approval. However, because these loans carry higher perceived risk, they often come with higher interest rates and stricter requirements in other areas. This makes them best suited for strategic use rather than as a primary financing method.

Choosing between these three loan types is not just a technical decision—it is a strategic one. The right choice depends on your goals, your financial profile, and the specifics of the property you are acquiring. If your property has strong income potential and meets DSCR requirements, a DSCR loan is often the most efficient and scalable option. If your property's income is less predictable or you want to leverage your personal cash flow, a bank statement loan may be more appropriate. If you have strong assets and need maximum flexibility, a no-doc loan can provide a powerful alternative.

Another important consideration is how these loan types impact your ability to scale. DSCR loans are generally the most scalable because they allow you to qualify based on each property individually, without being limited by your personal income. This means you can continue acquiring properties as long as each deal meets the lender's criteria. Bank statement loans, while flexible, still tie your borrowing capacity to your overall cash flow, which can create limitations as you grow. No-doc loans, while flexible in documentation, may require larger capital commitments, which can also impact scalability.

Interest rates and loan terms also vary between these options. DSCR loans typically offer competitive rates for investment properties, especially when the DSCR ratio is strong. Bank statement loans may have slightly higher rates due to the additional risk associated with income estimation. No-doc loans often have the highest rates, reflecting the lack of income verification. Understanding these differences is essential for evaluating the long-term profitability of your investments.

Risk management is another critical factor. Each loan type carries its own risk profile, both for the lender and the borrower. DSCR loans rely on property performance, which means your success depends on maintaining strong occupancy and pricing. Bank statement loans rely on consistent cash flow, which requires stable business operations. No-doc loans rely on your overall financial strength, which requires careful management of assets and reserves. By understanding these risks, you can make informed decisions and build a more resilient portfolio.

As you develop your investing strategy, you will likely use all three of these loan types at different stages. Early in your journey, you may rely more on bank statement loans to leverage your existing income. As you build a portfolio of income-producing properties, you may transition to DSCR loans for greater scalability. In certain situations, you may use no-doc loans to move quickly or simplify the process. The key is not to limit yourself to one approach, but to understand how each option fits into your overall strategy.

Ultimately, mastering these loan types gives you control. Instead of being constrained by a single method of qualification, you gain the ability to choose the best financing structure for each deal. This flexibility is one of the greatest advantages in Airbnb investing, where opportunities can vary widely in terms of location, performance, and timing. By aligning your financing strategy with each opportunity, you position yourself to move faster, make better decisions, and achieve greater long-term success.

Real-Life Math Example: Comparing DSCR, Bank Statement, and No-Doc Loan Scenarios

Consider an investor named David who is evaluating three different financing options for an Airbnb property priced at $600,000. He wants to understand how each loan type impacts his ability to qualify, his monthly payment, and his overall profitability.

In the DSCR scenario, David puts down 25%, or $150,000, resulting in a loan amount of $450,000. The interest rate is 7.25%, and the monthly principal and interest payment is approximately $3,070. Including taxes and insurance, the total monthly expense is $3,600. The lender requires a minimum DSCR of 1.20, meaning the property must generate at least $4,320 per month in rental income.

David analyzes Airbnb data and finds that the property has an average daily rate of $250 and an occupancy rate of 65%. At full occupancy, the monthly revenue would be $7,500. Applying the 65% occupancy rate, the projected monthly income is $4,875. Dividing this by the monthly expense of $3,600 results in a DSCR of approximately 1.35, which exceeds the lender's requirement. This means David qualifies for the loan based solely on the property's performance.

In the bank statement scenario, David uses 12 months of business bank statements showing total deposits of $240,000, or $20,000 per month. The lender applies a 50% expense factor, resulting in a qualifying income of $10,000 per month. With a maximum debt-to-income ratio of 50%, David can support monthly debt obligations of up to $5,000. Since the property's monthly expense is $3,600, he qualifies comfortably under this method as well.

However, the bank statement loan comes with a slightly higher interest rate of 7.75%, increasing the monthly payment to $3,250 for principal and interest, and $3,780 total with taxes and insurance. While David still qualifies, the higher payment reduces his cash flow compared to the DSCR option.

In the no-doc scenario, David puts down 30%, or $180,000, reducing the loan amount to $420,000. The interest rate is 8.25%, and the monthly principal and interest payment is approximately $3,150. Including taxes and insurance, the total monthly expense is $3,700. The lender does not require income verification, but requires a credit score above 740 and reserves of 12 months, or $44,400.

David meets these requirements, allowing him to secure the loan quickly. However, the higher down payment and interest rate reduce his leverage and overall return on investment. While this option provides flexibility, it may not be the most efficient choice for scaling.

Comparing the three scenarios, David sees that the DSCR loan offers the best balance of leverage, rate, and scalability, provided the property meets income requirements. The bank statement loan offers flexibility but at a higher cost. The no-doc loan offers speed and simplicity but requires more capital and comes with higher rates.

Through this analysis, David gains a clear understanding of how each loan type impacts his investment. He chooses the DSCR loan for this property, while keeping the other options available for future deals where conditions may differ. This strategic approach allows him to adapt to different opportunities and continue growing his Airbnb portfolio efficiently.

Chapter 3

Self-Employed Borrower Strategies for Airbnb Mortgage Approval

One of the most powerful advantages of no-income verification Airbnb mortgage loans is how well they align with the realities of self-employed borrowers. Entrepreneurs, business owners, freelancers, and investors often operate with income structures that do not fit traditional lending models. They may generate substantial revenue, yet show limited taxable income due to deductions, reinvestment, and strategic financial planning. This creates a disconnect between real financial strength and what lenders see on paper. In this chapter, you will learn how to bridge that gap and position yourself as a strong, qualified borrower—without relying on traditional income documentation.

The first mindset shift you must adopt is understanding that lenders are not rejecting self-employed borrowers—they are simply unable to evaluate them using outdated frameworks. When you remove tax returns from the equation, the question becomes: how else can you demonstrate stability, reliability, and the ability to manage debt? The answer lies in a combination of credit strength, liquidity, deal structure, and property performance. These are the pillars that replace traditional income verification, and mastering them allows you to compete at a high level in the Airbnb investment space.

One of the most important strategies for self-employed borrowers is separating personal income from investment qualification. Many entrepreneurs make the mistake of trying to "prove" their income through documentation, even when better options exist. Instead, the goal should be to use loan programs—such as DSCR loans—that focus on the property's income rather than the borrower's. This allows you to bypass the limitations created by tax returns and focus on what truly matters: whether the property can support itself financially. By thinking in terms of deal qualification instead of personal qualification, you unlock a more scalable and efficient path forward.

Another critical strategy is optimizing your credit profile. For self-employed borrowers, credit often becomes the primary indicator of financial responsibility in the absence of traditional income documentation. Lenders view strong credit as evidence that you consistently meet your obligations, even if your income structure is complex. This means that improving your credit score—even by a small margin—can significantly impact your loan options, interest rates, and approval likelihood. Strategic actions such as reducing credit card utilization, avoiding unnecessary inquiries, and maintaining a perfect payment history can elevate your profile and open doors to better financing.

Liquidity is equally important, and in many cases, it becomes the deciding factor in loan approval. Lenders want to see that you have sufficient funds to handle mortgage payments, property expenses, and unexpected challenges. For self-employed borrowers, this often means maintaining higher reserves than traditional borrowers. These reserves are not just a requirement—they are a signal of stability. By demonstrating that you have the financial capacity to support your investments, you reduce the lender's perceived risk and strengthen your overall application.

Business structuring also plays a key role in your strategy. Many Airbnb investors operate through LLCs or other business entities, which can provide liability protection and operational flexibility. However, the way these entities are structured—and how funds flow between them—can impact your ability to qualify for loans. For example, commingling personal and business finances can create confusion during underwriting, while maintaining clear separation can enhance your credibility. Understanding how to present your financial picture in a clean, organized manner is essential for building lender confidence. Another often-overlooked strategy is timing. Self-employed borrowers have more control over their financial presentation than they realize. The timing of large deposits, major expenses, and account balances can influence how lenders perceive your stability. For example, maintaining consistent account balances and avoiding sudden fluctuations can create a more favorable impression. Similarly, ensuring that your reserves are fully seasoned—meaning they have been in your accounts for a sufficient period—can prevent delays or complications during the approval process.

Property selection is also a strategic decision for self-employed investors. Since many no-income verification loans rely heavily on property performance, choosing the right property becomes critical. This means analyzing not just location and appreciation potential, but also income metrics such as average daily rate, occupancy, and seasonal trends. A property that meets or exceeds DSCR requirements can effectively replace the need for personal income documentation, making it easier to secure financing and scale your portfolio.

In addition to selecting the right property, you must also understand how to present that property to the lender. This includes providing accurate and well-supported rental projections, using reliable data sources, and highlighting comparable properties that demonstrate strong performance. The goal is to build a clear and compelling case that the property is a sound investment capable of generating consistent income. This level of preparation can make a significant difference in the approval process.

Self-employed borrowers can also benefit from layering multiple strategies together. For example, you may use a DSCR loan as your primary qualification method while also demonstrating strong reserves and credit. In some cases, you may combine elements of bank statement analysis with property performance to create a more comprehensive profile. The key is flexibility—understanding that there is no single path to approval, but rather a range of options that can be tailored to your specific situation.

Another advanced strategy involves planning for future scalability. Many self-employed investors focus solely on getting approved for their next deal, without considering how their current decisions will impact future opportunities. For example, using too much liquidity on a single deal may limit your ability to acquire additional properties. Similarly, choosing a loan structure that ties your qualification to personal income may create bottlenecks as you grow. By thinking ahead and structuring your deals strategically, you can create a system that supports continuous expansion.

Risk management is also an essential component of your strategy. While no-income verification loans offer flexibility, they also require a disciplined approach to investing. This means maintaining adequate reserves, selecting properties with strong and stable income potential, and avoiding over-leverage. Self-employed borrowers, in particular, must be mindful of income variability and ensure that their investments can withstand fluctuations in occupancy or market conditions. By managing risk effectively, you not only protect your portfolio but also enhance your long-term credibility with lenders.

As you develop these strategies, you will begin to see that self-employment is not a disadvantage—it is an opportunity. It gives you the flexibility to structure your finances in a way that aligns with your investing goals. It allows you to take advantage of loan programs designed for investors rather than employees. And it enables you to build a portfolio based on performance, strategy, and control rather than rigid income requirements.

The most successful Airbnb investors who are self-employed understand that their financial profile is something they can shape and optimize. They do not rely on a single method of qualification. Instead, they build a comprehensive strategy that includes credit optimization, liquidity management, property selection, and deal structuring. This holistic approach allows them to navigate the lending landscape with confidence and achieve results that would be difficult under traditional financing models.

Ultimately, the goal is not just to get approved—it is to create a repeatable system for success. By mastering the strategies outlined in this chapter, you position yourself to acquire properties consistently, scale your portfolio efficiently, and operate with a level of flexibility that sets you apart from other investors. This is the true power of no-income verification lending for self-employed borrowers: the ability to turn complexity into an advantage and build a business that grows on your terms.

Real-Life Math Example: Self-Employed Borrower Structuring an Airbnb Deal

Consider an investor named Michael, a self-employed entrepreneur who owns multiple online businesses. His annual revenue is $300,000, but after deductions and write-offs, his taxable income shows only $70,000. Under traditional lending guidelines, this significantly limits his borrowing capacity. However, Michael decides to pursue a DSCR loan to acquire an Airbnb property valued at $550,000.

Michael plans to put down 25%, which equals $137,500, resulting in a loan amount of $412,500. The interest rate is 7.5%, and the monthly principal and interest payment is approximately $2,880. When adding taxes and insurance, the total monthly housing expense comes to $3,300.

The lender requires a minimum DSCR of 1.20. To meet this requirement, the property must generate at least $3,960 per month in rental income. Michael researches comparable Airbnb properties in the area and finds that similar homes have an average daily rate of $230 and an occupancy rate of 68%.

At full occupancy, the property could generate $6,900 per month ($230 multiplied by 30 days). Applying the 68% occupancy rate, the projected monthly income is $4,692. Dividing this by the monthly expense of $3,300 results in a DSCR of approximately 1.42, which exceeds the lender's requirement.

In addition to meeting the DSCR requirement, Michael strengthens his application by demonstrating strong reserves. The lender requires six months of reserves, which equals $19,800 ($3,300 multiplied by 6). Michael has $50,000 in liquid funds after closing, which significantly exceeds the requirement and positions him as a low-risk borrower.

Michael's credit score is 735, allowing him to secure competitive loan terms. If his score were below 700, he might face a higher interest rate or stricter requirements. By maintaining strong credit, he enhances his approval odds and reduces his borrowing costs. Now consider how Michael might have approached this deal using a bank statement loan. His average monthly deposits are $25,000. After applying a 50% expense factor, his qualifying income is $12,500 per month. With a maximum debt-to-income ratio of 50%, he could support monthly debt obligations of up to $6,250. While this would allow him to qualify for the loan, the interest rate would likely be higher—around 7.875%—increasing his monthly payment and reducing cash flow.

By choosing the DSCR loan, Michael avoids the need to document his income and secures a more efficient financing structure. His projected monthly income of $4,692 minus expenses of $3,300 results in a positive cash flow of $1,392 per month. Over time, he plans to increase the average daily rate to $250 and improve occupancy to 72%, raising his monthly income to approximately $5,400 and further increasing cash flow.

This example demonstrates how a self-employed borrower can leverage property performance, credit, and reserves to qualify for financing without relying on tax returns. By understanding the numbers and applying the right strategy, Michael is able to acquire a high-performing Airbnb property and position himself for future growth.

Chapter 4

Credit and Reserve Positioning for No-Income Verification Airbnb Loans

When you remove traditional income documentation from the mortgage approval process, two factors immediately rise to the top as primary decision drivers: credit and reserves. These are no longer secondary considerations—they become the foundation of your borrower profile. In no-income verification Airbnb lending, your credit tells the lender how reliably you handle debt, while your reserves demonstrate your ability to sustain that debt over time. Together, they form a powerful combination that can either strengthen or weaken your entire deal, regardless of how strong the property itself may be.

The first concept to understand is that credit is not just a number—it is a story. Every payment you have made, every balance you carry, and every account you manage contributes to a narrative about your financial behavior. Lenders interpret this narrative to assess risk. In the absence of tax returns and income verification, this story becomes even more important. A borrower with a strong credit profile signals consistency, discipline, and reliability. These qualities can offset other perceived risks and open the door to better loan terms, including lower interest rates, higher loan-to-value ratios, and more flexible approval conditions.

For Airbnb investors using no-income verification loans, credit thresholds are often higher than traditional loan programs. While some lenders may accept scores in the mid-600s, the most competitive terms are typically reserved for borrowers with scores above 700 or even 720. This means that small improvements in your credit score can have a significant impact on your financing options. For example, increasing your score from 695 to 720 may reduce your interest rate, lower your required reserves, and improve your overall approval profile. Understanding this leverage is critical, because it allows you to treat credit improvement as an investment rather than an afterthought.

One of the most effective ways to optimize your credit is by managing utilization. Credit utilization refers to the percentage of your available credit that you are currently using. High utilization can signal financial stress, even if you are making payments on time. By reducing your balances and keeping utilization below key thresholds—such as 30%, 20%, or even 10%—you can improve your score relatively quickly. This is one of the fastest ways to enhance your borrower profile before applying for a loan. Another important factor is payment history, which carries significant weight in credit scoring models. Consistently making on-time payments demonstrates reliability and builds trust with lenders. Even a single late payment can have a noticeable impact on your score, especially in the context of no-income verification loans where credit plays a larger role. For this reason, maintaining a perfect or near-perfect payment history is essential if you want to access the best financing options.

The age and diversity of your credit accounts also contribute to your overall profile. A longer credit history provides more data for lenders to evaluate, while a mix of account types—such as credit cards, installment loans, and lines of credit—demonstrates your ability to manage different forms of debt. While these factors may not have the same immediate impact as utilization or payment history, they play an important role in building a strong, well-rounded credit profile over time.

While credit tells the story of your past behavior, reserves tell the story of your future stability. Reserves are the funds you have available after closing to cover mortgage payments and property expenses. In no-income verification lending, reserves serve as a safety net that reassures lenders you can handle fluctuations in income, unexpected repairs, or temporary vacancies. This is especially important for Airbnb properties, where income can vary based on seasonality, market conditions, and operational performance.

Reserve requirements vary depending on the loan program, property type, and borrower profile. Many DSCR and no-doc loans require between three and twelve months of reserves, calculated based on the total monthly housing expense. This includes principal, interest, taxes, insurance, and sometimes association fees. For example, if your total monthly payment is $3,000 and the lender requires six months of reserves, you would need to demonstrate at least $18,000 in available funds after closing.

However, meeting the minimum requirement is only part of the strategy. Stronger reserves can significantly enhance your application and improve your negotiating position. Lenders view higher reserves as a sign of financial strength and may offer better terms to borrowers who exceed the minimum. In some cases, additional reserves can compensate for other factors, such as a lower DSCR or a higher loan-to-value ratio. This makes reserve building a critical component of your overall financing strategy.

It is also important to understand what qualifies as reserves. Typically, lenders accept liquid or near-liquid assets such as cash in checking or savings accounts, money market funds, and certain investment accounts. Retirement accounts may also be considered, although they are often discounted to account for potential penalties or restrictions. The key is that these funds must be accessible and verifiable. Understanding how to structure and present your assets can make a significant difference in how your application is evaluated.

Timing and seasoning of reserves are additional factors to consider. Lenders prefer to see funds that have been in your accounts for a consistent period, rather than recently deposited large sums that may raise questions. This is known as seasoning, and it helps demonstrate that your reserves are stable and not borrowed or temporary. Planning ahead and maintaining consistent balances can prevent delays and strengthen your overall profile.

Another advanced strategy involves aligning your credit and reserve positioning with your long-term investment goals. For example, using all your available cash for a large down payment may reduce your reserves and limit your ability to acquire additional properties. Conversely, maintaining higher reserves may allow you to pursue multiple deals simultaneously. Balancing these factors requires a strategic approach that considers both immediate and future opportunities.

Credit and reserves also play a critical role in risk management. While no-income verification loans provide flexibility, they also require a disciplined approach to financial planning. Strong credit reduces borrowing costs and increases access to capital, while adequate reserves provide a buffer against uncertainty. Together, they create a stable foundation that supports sustainable growth. Without this foundation, even the best investment opportunities can become risky.

As you continue to build your Airbnb portfolio, you will find that credit and reserves are not static—they are dynamic tools that can be adjusted and optimized over time. You may choose to pay down debt to improve your credit score, or strategically build reserves in anticipation of future acquisitions. By actively managing these elements, you maintain control over your financing options and position yourself to take advantage of new opportunities as they arise.

Ultimately, credit and reserve positioning are about more than just getting approved—they are about creating leverage. Strong credit allows you to access better terms, while strong reserves provide the confidence to pursue larger and more complex deals. Together, they give you the flexibility to operate strategically rather than reactively. This is what separates successful investors from those who struggle to scale.

By mastering the principles outlined in this chapter, you will be able to present yourself as a low-risk, high-confidence borrower, even without traditional income documentation. You will understand how to optimize your credit, build and maintain reserves, and align these factors with your investment strategy. This knowledge will not only improve your approval odds but also enhance your ability to grow your Airbnb portfolio in a controlled and sustainable way.

Real-Life Math Example: Credit and Reserve Positioning in an Airbnb Loan

Consider an investor named Lisa who is purchasing an Airbnb property for $650,000 using a DSCR loan. She plans to put down 25%, which equals $162,500, resulting in a loan amount of $487,500. The interest rate she is offered depends on her credit score. With a score of 680, her rate would be 8.0%, resulting in a monthly principal and interest payment of approximately $3,580. With taxes and insurance, her total monthly expense would be $4,200.

However, Lisa improves her credit score to 720 before applying for the loan. This allows her to secure a lower interest rate of 7.25%, reducing her monthly principal and interest payment to approximately $3,330. With taxes and insurance, her total monthly expense becomes $3,950. This difference of

$250 per month translates to $3,000 per year in savings, demonstrating the financial impact of credit optimization.

The lender requires a minimum DSCR of 1.20, meaning the property must generate at least $4,740 per month in rental income ($3,950 multiplied by 1.20). Lisa analyzes the market and finds that the property can achieve an average daily rate of $260 with a 70% occupancy rate. At full occupancy, the monthly revenue would be $7,800. Applying the occupancy rate, the projected monthly income is $5,460.

Dividing $5,460 by the monthly expense of $3,950 results in a DSCR of approximately 1.38, which exceeds the lender's requirement. This confirms that the property qualifies based on its income performance.

Next, Lisa evaluates her reserve requirements. The lender requires six months of reserves, which equals $23,700 ($3,950 multiplied by 6). Lisa has $40,000 in liquid funds after closing, exceeding the requirement by $16,300. This not only satisfies the lender's criteria but also strengthens her application and positions her for better terms.

Now consider an alternative scenario where Lisa uses a larger down payment of 30%, or $195,000, reducing her loan amount to $455,000. This lowers her monthly expense to approximately $3,700. Her required DSCR income becomes

$4,440, making it easier to qualify. However, using more cash for the down payment reduces her remaining reserves to $25,000, which is just above the minimum requirement. This illustrates the trade-off between leverage and liquidity. By analyzing these scenarios, Lisa determines that maintaining stronger reserves while optimizing her credit provides the best overall outcome. She chooses the 25% down payment option, preserves more liquidity, and benefits from the lower interest rate achieved through her improved credit score.

This example highlights how credit and reserves work together to shape the outcome of a no-income verification loan. By understanding the numbers and making strategic decisions, Lisa is able to secure favorable financing terms, maintain financial flexibility, and position herself for future investments.

Chapter 5

Structuring the Deal for Maximum Approval and Profitability

At this stage in your journey, you understand the core components of no-income verification Airbnb lending: DSCR, bank statement options, credit positioning, and reserves. Now it is time to bring everything together into one of the most important skills you can develop as an investor—the ability to structure a deal. Deal structuring is where strategy meets execution. It is the process of aligning the property, the loan, and your financial profile in a way that not only gets you approved, but also maximizes your long-term profitability and scalability.

The first principle of deal structuring is understanding that approval is not binary—it is flexible. Many investors believe that a deal either works or it does not, but in reality, most deals can be adjusted to meet lender requirements. This may involve changing the down payment, selecting a different loan program, improving the property's projected income, or strengthening your borrower profile. The key is to approach each deal with a problem-solving mindset rather than a pass-or-fail mentality.

One of the most powerful levers you have in structuring a deal is the loan-to-value ratio. The amount you choose to put down directly impacts your approval odds, your monthly payment, and your overall return on investment. A higher down payment reduces risk for the lender, making it easier to qualify, especially if the property's DSCR is borderline. However, it also ties up more capital, which could limit your ability to pursue additional deals. Conversely, a lower down payment increases leverage and potential returns, but may require stronger credit, higher reserves, or a higher-performing property to offset the increased risk.

Another critical element is interest rate selection and loan terms. Even small differences in interest rates can have a significant impact on your monthly payment and long-term profitability. In no-income verification lending, rates can vary based on credit score, DSCR ratio, reserves, and overall borrower strength. By optimizing these factors, you can position yourself for more favorable terms. Additionally, understanding options such as interest-only periods or adjustable-rate structures can provide flexibility in managing cash flow, particularly in the early stages of an investment.

Property income is at the heart of Airbnb deal structuring, especially when using DSCR loans. This means that your ability to analyze and optimize rental performance is just as important as your ability to secure financing. Factors such as average daily rate, occupancy, seasonality, and guest experience all influence the property's income potential. By selecting properties with strong fundamentals and implementing effective management strategies, you can increase your DSCR ratio and improve both approval odds and profitability.

It is also important to consider expense management as part of your deal structure. While increasing revenue is critical, controlling expenses can have an equally powerful effect on your bottom line. This includes property taxes, insurance, maintenance, cleaning costs, and platform fees. By accurately estimating and managing these expenses, you can ensure that your projections are realistic and that your investment remains profitable over time. Lenders will often evaluate these factors as part of their risk assessment, making accuracy and transparency essential.

Another advanced strategy in deal structuring is the use of buffers. Instead of aiming to meet the minimum DSCR requirement, successful investors build in a margin of safety. For example, if a lender requires a DSCR of 1.20, you might target 1.30 or higher. This buffer protects you against fluctuations in income and provides additional confidence to the lender. It also creates a more resilient investment that can withstand changes in market conditions, such as lower occupancy or increased competition.

Timing and market conditions also play a role in how you structure your deal. Interest rates, property values, and rental demand can all influence the viability of an investment. Understanding these dynamics allows you to adjust your strategy accordingly. For example, in a higher interest rate environment, you may need to focus more on properties with strong cash flow to maintain acceptable DSCR levels. In a lower rate environment, you may have more flexibility to prioritize appreciation and long-term growth.

One of the most overlooked aspects of deal structuring is exit strategy planning. Before you even close on a property, you should have a clear understanding of how you plan to use it in the future. Will you hold it for long-term cash flow, refinance to pull out equity, or sell it for a profit? Each of these strategies has implications for how you structure the deal initially. For example, maintaining strong DSCR and reserves can position you for a future cash-out refinance, allowing you to recycle capital and scale your portfolio more quickly.

Another key consideration is how each deal fits into your broader portfolio strategy. Successful investors do not evaluate properties in isolation—they consider how each acquisition contributes to their overall goals. This includes balancing high-cash-flow properties with those that offer strong appreciation potential, managing risk across different markets, and ensuring that liquidity is preserved for future opportunities. By thinking holistically, you can create a portfolio that is both profitable and sustainable.

Leverage is one of the most powerful tools in real estate investing, but it must be used carefully. While higher leverage can increase returns, it also increases risk. In the context of no-income verification loans, where income variability is a factor, it is important to strike a balance between maximizing returns and maintaining stability. This often involves making strategic decisions about down payments, loan structures, and reserve levels to ensure that your portfolio can withstand unexpected challenges.

Negotiation is another important component of deal structuring. This includes negotiating the purchase price, seller concessions, and even loan terms. For example, securing a lower purchase price can improve your DSCR ratio and increase your margin of safety. Similarly, negotiating credits or concessions can reduce your upfront costs and preserve liquidity. These factors can have a significant impact on the overall success of your investment. As you refine your approach to deal structuring, you will begin to see patterns and opportunities that others may overlook. You will recognize how small adjustments can transform a marginal deal into a strong one, and how strategic thinking can unlock financing options that might otherwise seem out of reach. This level of insight is what allows experienced investors to move quickly and confidently in competitive markets.

Ultimately, structuring the deal is about control. It is about taking all the variables—property, financing, credit, reserves, and strategy—and aligning them in a way that supports your goals. When done correctly, it allows you to not only secure approval, but to build a portfolio that generates consistent cash flow, grows in value, and provides long-term financial freedom.

By mastering the principles in this chapter, you will develop the ability to evaluate opportunities with precision, structure deals with confidence, and execute your strategy effectively. This is the skill that turns knowledge into results and transforms individual transactions into a scalable, profitable business.

Real-Life Math Example: Structuring an Airbnb Deal for Approval and Profit

Consider an investor named Daniel who is evaluating an Airbnb property listed at $700,000. He wants to structure the deal in a way that maximizes both approval odds and long-term profitability using a DSCR loan. Daniel initially considers a 20% down payment, or $140,000, resulting in a loan amount of $560,000. At an interest rate of 7.5%, his monthly principal and interest payment would be approximately $3,920. Adding taxes and insurance brings the total monthly expense to $4,600. The lender requires a minimum DSCR of 1.20, meaning the property must generate at least $5,520 per month in rental income.

Daniel analyzes the property's potential and estimates an average daily rate of $275 with an occupancy rate of 65%. At full occupancy, the monthly revenue would be $8,250. Applying the occupancy rate, the projected monthly income is $5,362. This results in a DSCR of approximately 1.17, which falls short of the lender's requirement.

Instead of abandoning the deal, Daniel adjusts the structure. He increases his down payment to 25%, or $175,000, reducing the loan amount to $525,000. This lowers his monthly principal and interest payment to approximately $3,680, and his total monthly expense to $4,300. The required DSCR income becomes $5,160.

With the same projected income of $5,362, the DSCR now increases to approximately 1.25, exceeding the lender's requirement. This adjustment transforms the deal from unqualified to approved.

Daniel also explores ways to improve the property's performance. By implementing professional staging, dynamic pricing, and optimized listings, he believes he can increase the average daily rate to $290 and occupancy to 68%. This would raise monthly income to approximately $5,916, further improving the DSCR and increasing cash flow.

Next, Daniel evaluates his reserves. The lender requires six months of reserves, which equals $25,800 ($4,300 multiplied by 6). Daniel ensures he has $60,000 in liquid funds after closing, providing a strong financial cushion and enhancing his application.

Finally, Daniel calculates his projected cash flow. With an estimated monthly income of $5,916 and expenses of $4,300, he expects a positive cash flow of $1,616 per month. Over a year, this equates to $19,392 in pre-tax cash flow.

By adjusting his down payment, optimizing property performance, and maintaining strong reserves, Daniel successfully structures the deal for both approval and profitability. This example demonstrates how strategic thinking and attention to detail can turn a borderline deal into a successful investment while positioning the investor for future growth.

Chapter 6

Scaling Your Airbnb Portfolio Using No-Income Verification Loans

Once you understand how to qualify for a single Airbnb property using no-income verification strategies, the next level is learning how to scale. Scaling is where real wealth is created in real estate. It is not about owning one successful property—it is about building a system that allows you to acquire multiple income-producing assets over time while maintaining control, stability, and profitability. In the context of Airbnb investing, scaling requires a combination of financing strategy, operational efficiency, and long-term planning.

The first concept to understand is that scaling is not simply about buying more properties—it is about building a repeatable process. This process includes identifying high-performing markets, selecting the right properties, structuring deals effectively, and securing financing in a way that does not limit your future growth. No-income verification loans, particularly DSCR loans, play a central role in this process because they allow you to qualify based on each property's performance rather than your personal income.

This removes one of the biggest bottlenecks in traditional lending and opens the door to portfolio expansion.

One of the most powerful aspects of DSCR-based scaling is that each property stands on its own. This means that your ability to acquire additional properties is not directly tied to your personal income or existing debt obligations. As long as each new property meets the lender's DSCR requirements and you maintain strong credit and reserves, you can continue to grow your portfolio. This creates a scalable model that is particularly well-suited for Airbnb investing, where properties can generate higher income than traditional rentals.

However, scaling also introduces new challenges. As you acquire more properties, your exposure to market fluctuations, operational complexity, and financial risk increases. This makes it essential to approach scaling with a structured and disciplined strategy. One of the key elements of this strategy is maintaining strong liquidity. While it may be tempting to deploy all available capital into new acquisitions, doing so can leave you vulnerable to unexpected expenses or temporary declines in income. Maintaining adequate reserves across your portfolio ensures that you can weather these challenges without disrupting your growth.

Another important factor in scaling is portfolio diversification. Relying on a single market or property type can increase risk, especially in the Airbnb space where regulations, seasonality, and competition can vary significantly. By diversifying across different locations and property types, you reduce your exposure to localized risks and create a more stable income stream. This also provides flexibility in financing, as different markets may offer different opportunities for DSCR qualification and loan structures.

Operational efficiency is another critical component of scaling. Managing one Airbnb property is relatively straightforward, but managing multiple properties requires systems and processes. This includes standardizing your listing setup, pricing strategies, guest communication, cleaning operations, and maintenance. By creating repeatable systems, you can maintain consistent performance across your portfolio and maximize income potential. This is particularly important for DSCR loans, where property performance directly impacts your ability to qualify for additional financing.

Financing strategy becomes even more important as you scale. While DSCR loans are often the primary tool, you may also incorporate other loan types depending on the situation. For example, you might use bank statement loans to leverage personal cash flow in certain scenarios, or no-doc loans to move quickly on time-sensitive opportunities. The key is to remain flexible and use each financing option strategically. This allows you to adapt to different deals and market conditions while maintaining momentum. Another advanced strategy for scaling is the use of refinancing and equity extraction. As your properties increase in value and generate consistent income, you may be able to refinance them and pull out equity. This capital can then be reinvested into additional properties, creating a cycle of growth often referred to as "equity recycling." In the Airbnb space, where properties can appreciate and generate strong cash flow, this strategy can significantly accelerate portfolio expansion.

It is also important to consider the role of leverage in scaling. Leverage allows you to control larger assets with less capital, increasing your potential returns. However, it also increases risk, particularly in a variable income environment like Airbnb. Successful investors understand how to balance leverage with stability. This often involves maintaining conservative DSCR ratios, strong reserves, and a diversified portfolio. By managing leverage carefully, you can scale your portfolio while minimizing downside risk.

Another key element of scaling is understanding lender limits and guidelines. While DSCR loans offer flexibility, lenders may have limits on the number of financed properties, exposure per borrower, or total loan amounts. Building relationships with multiple lenders can help you navigate these limits and continue growing your portfolio. Each lender may have slightly different criteria, and understanding these nuances allows you to match each deal with the most appropriate financing source.

Time management and decision-making also become more critical as you scale. Opportunities in the Airbnb market can move quickly, and the ability to evaluate deals efficiently is a competitive advantage. This requires a clear set of criteria for what constitutes a good investment, including target DSCR ratios, cash flow thresholds, and risk tolerance. By establishing these criteria in advance, you can make faster and more confident decisions.

Another often overlooked aspect of scaling is the importance of data. Tracking the performance of your properties—occupancy rates, average daily rates, expenses, and cash flow—provides valuable insights that can inform future decisions. This data allows you to identify trends, optimize performance, and refine your strategy over time. It also strengthens your position when working with lenders, as you can demonstrate a track record of successful investments.

As your portfolio grows, you may also explore partnerships or additional funding sources. While no-income verification loans reduce reliance on personal income, combining your expertise with additional capital can further accelerate growth. This might involve working with partners, private lenders, or other investors. Structuring these relationships effectively is an advanced strategy that can expand your capacity while maintaining control over your investments.

Ultimately, scaling your Airbnb portfolio is about creating momentum. Each successful deal builds on the previous one, increasing your experience, your capital base, and your ability to secure financing. By leveraging no-income verification loans, you remove traditional barriers and create a pathway for continuous growth. However, this growth must be managed carefully to ensure that it is sustainable and aligned with your long-term goals.

The investors who succeed at scaling are those who combine strategic thinking with disciplined execution. They understand how to structure deals, manage risk, and optimize performance. They build systems that allow them to operate efficiently and make decisions with confidence. Most importantly, they view each property not as an isolated investment, but as part of a larger system designed to generate income and create wealth.

By applying the principles in this chapter, you will be able to move beyond individual transactions and begin building a true portfolio. You will understand how to use financing strategically, manage your resources effectively, and scale your investments in a way that supports long-term success. This is where the real power of Airbnb investing and no-income verification lending comes together—creating opportunities that grow with you over time.

Real-Life Math Example: Scaling from One Airbnb Property to a Portfolio

Consider an investor named Alex who starts with a single Airbnb property purchased for $500,000 using a DSCR loan. He puts down 25%, or $125,000, resulting in a loan amount of $375,000. At an interest rate of 7.5%, his monthly principal and interest payment is approximately $2,620. Including taxes and insurance, his total monthly expense is $3,100.

The property generates an average daily rate of $220 with a 70% occupancy rate. At full occupancy, monthly revenue would be $6,600. Applying the occupancy rate, the actual monthly income is $4,620. This results in a DSCR of approximately 1.49 and a monthly cash flow of $1,520.

After one year, Alex has generated approximately $18,240 in cash flow. In addition, the property has appreciated by 5%, increasing its value to $525,000. He decides to refinance and pull out equity. With a new loan at 75% of the updated value, he can access approximately $393,750. After paying off the original loan balance, he extracts around $40,000 in usable capital. Alex combines this $40,000 with additional savings to fund the down payment on a second property priced at $600,000. He follows a similar structure, putting down 25% and securing a DSCR loan. The second property generates $5,200 per month in income with expenses of $3,800, resulting in a DSCR of approximately 1.37 and a monthly cash flow of $1,400.

Now with two properties, Alex's total monthly cash flow is approximately $2,920. Over another year, he accumulates additional savings and observes appreciation in both properties. He repeats the refinancing process, extracting equity and using it to acquire a third property priced at $700,000.

The third property generates $6,000 per month in income with expenses of $4,400, resulting in a DSCR of approximately 1.36 and a monthly cash flow of $1,600. At this point, Alex owns three properties generating a combined monthly cash flow of approximately $4,520, or $54,240 annually.

By continuing this cycle—acquiring, optimizing, refinancing, and reinvesting—Alex is able to scale his portfolio over time. Each property contributes to his overall income and provides additional leverage for future acquisitions. Importantly, he is able to do this without relying on traditional income verification, instead using property performance, credit, and reserves to qualify for each loan. This example illustrates how scaling works in practice. It is not about making one large leap, but about taking consistent, strategic steps that build on each other. By understanding the numbers and applying the right strategies, Alex transforms a single property into a growing portfolio that generates increasing income and long-term wealth.

Chapter 7

Risk Management and Long-Term Stability in Airbnb No-Income Verification Investing

As you begin to scale your Airbnb portfolio using no-income verification loans, one of the most important shifts you must make is from growth-focused thinking to sustainability-focused thinking. Growth creates opportunity, but risk management preserves it. Many investors are able to acquire properties, but far fewer are able to hold, stabilize, and scale them over the long term. This chapter is about ensuring that everything you build is protected, optimized, and designed to last.

The first principle of risk management in Airbnb investing is understanding income variability. Unlike long-term rental properties with fixed lease agreements, Airbnb properties operate in a dynamic environment where income can fluctuate based on seasonality, local demand, competition, economic conditions, and even platform algorithm changes. This variability is both an opportunity and a risk. While it allows for higher income potential, it also requires careful planning to ensure that your properties remain profitable during slower periods. To manage this variability, you must adopt a conservative underwriting mindset. This means not relying solely on best-case projections, but instead analyzing realistic and even worst-case scenarios. For example, if a property performs at 75% occupancy during peak seasons, you might underwrite it at 60–65% occupancy to create a buffer. Similarly, you might use slightly lower average daily rates in your projections to ensure that your DSCR remains strong even if market conditions change. This approach reduces the likelihood of financial stress and increases the resilience of your portfolio.

Another critical element of risk management is maintaining strong DSCR ratios across your properties. While lenders may allow DSCR levels as low as 1.0 or slightly below in some cases, experienced investors aim for higher ratios—often 1.25 or above. This provides a margin of safety that protects against fluctuations in income. A higher DSCR not only improves loan approval odds but also ensures that your properties generate sufficient cash flow to cover expenses and contribute to your overall financial stability.

Reserves play a central role in managing risk. As discussed in previous chapters, reserves are your financial safety net. However, in the context of a growing Airbnb portfolio, reserves must be viewed at both the individual property level and the portfolio level. Each property should have sufficient reserves to cover its own expenses, but you should also maintain a broader reserve pool that can be used to support your entire portfolio if needed. This layered approach provides additional protection and flexibility.

Diversification is another key strategy for reducing risk. By spreading your investments across different markets, property types, and price points, you reduce your exposure to localized risks. For example, a change in regulations in one city may impact your ability to operate short-term rentals in that market. If all your properties are concentrated in that area, your entire portfolio could be affected. By diversifying, you create multiple income streams that are less likely to be impacted simultaneously.

Operational risk is also a significant factor in Airbnb investing. As you scale, managing multiple properties becomes more complex. Issues such as guest communication, cleaning coordination, maintenance, and pricing adjustments require efficient systems and processes. Without proper management, operational inefficiencies can lead to lower occupancy, reduced guest satisfaction, and ultimately decreased income. Investing in systems, tools, and potentially professional management can help mitigate these risks and maintain consistent performance. Market risk is another consideration that must be addressed. Real estate markets are influenced by a wide range of factors, including interest rates, economic conditions, and local supply and demand. In the Airbnb space, additional factors such as tourism trends and travel behavior can also impact performance. Staying informed about market conditions and adjusting your strategy accordingly is essential for long-term success. This may involve shifting your focus to different markets, adjusting pricing strategies, or even converting properties to long-term rentals if necessary.

Financing risk is particularly important when using no-income verification loans. While these loans provide flexibility, they often come with higher interest rates and stricter requirements in other areas. Changes in interest rates can impact your cash flow, especially if you are using adjustable-rate loans. Understanding the terms of your loans and planning for potential changes is critical. In some cases, locking in fixed rates or refinancing at the right time can help manage this risk.

Another important aspect of risk management is avoiding over-leverage. While leverage is a powerful tool for scaling, excessive leverage can increase vulnerability to market fluctuations. If your properties are highly leveraged and experience a decline in income, you may struggle to cover expenses. Maintaining a balanced approach—where leverage is used strategically but not excessively—helps ensure that your portfolio remains stable even during challenging periods.

Insurance and legal protection are also essential components of a comprehensive risk management strategy. Short-term rental properties may require specialized insurance policies that cover guest-related risks, property damage, and liability. Additionally, operating within local regulations and maintaining proper licensing is critical to avoid fines or operational disruptions. These protections may seem like additional costs, but they are essential investments in the longevity of your portfolio.

Another advanced strategy involves stress testing your portfolio. This means evaluating how your properties would perform under different scenarios, such as lower occupancy rates, reduced pricing, or increased expenses. By running these scenarios, you can identify potential weaknesses and make adjustments before issues arise. This proactive approach allows you to manage risk more effectively and maintain confidence in your investment strategy.

Cash flow management is also a key factor in long-term stability. Positive cash flow provides the flexibility to reinvest, build reserves, and absorb unexpected costs. However, it is important to track and manage this cash flow carefully. This includes monitoring income and expenses, setting aside funds for maintenance and upgrades, and ensuring that your properties remain competitive in the market. Strong cash flow management supports both growth and stability.

As your portfolio grows, you must also consider the human element of risk management. Decision fatigue, overextension, and lack of focus can all impact your ability to manage your investments effectively. Building a team, delegating responsibilities, and maintaining clear systems can help reduce these risks and allow you to operate more efficiently. This is especially important as the complexity of your portfolio increases.

Ultimately, risk management is about balance. It is about finding the right combination of growth and stability, leverage and liquidity, opportunity and protection. By approaching your investments with a disciplined and strategic mindset, you can build a portfolio that not only grows but endures. This is what separates short-term success from long-term wealth.

The goal is not to eliminate risk entirely—that is impossible. Instead, the goal is to understand, manage, and mitigate risk in a way that allows you to continue moving forward with confidence. By applying the principles in this chapter, you will be able to protect your investments, navigate challenges, and build a portfolio that stands the test of time.

Real-Life Math Example: Stress Testing and Risk Management in an Airbnb Portfolio

Consider an investor named Kevin who owns three Airbnb properties. Each property was financed using DSCR loans and generates positive cash flow under normal conditions. Kevin wants to evaluate how his portfolio would perform under different scenarios to ensure long-term stability.

Property 1 generates $4,800 per month in income with expenses of $3,200, resulting in a DSCR of 1.50 and a cash flow of $1,600. Property 2 generates $5,200 per month with expenses of $3,800, resulting in a DSCR of 1.37 and a cash flow of $1,400. Property 3 generates $6,000 per month with expenses of $4,500, resulting in a DSCR of 1.33 and a cash flow of $1,500. Combined, Kevin's portfolio generates $16,000 in monthly income with total expenses of $11,500, resulting in a combined cash flow of $4,500.

Kevin decides to stress test his portfolio by reducing occupancy rates by 15%, which lowers his income across all properties. Property 1's income drops to $4,080, Property 2's income drops to $4,420, and Property 3's income drops to $5,100. The new total monthly income is $13,600.

With expenses remaining at $11,500, Kevin's new combined cash flow is $2,100. While this is a significant reduction, his portfolio remains cash flow positive. His DSCR ratios also decrease but remain above 1.0, indicating that the properties can still cover their expenses.

Next, Kevin evaluates a more severe scenario where both occupancy and average daily rates decline, resulting in a 25% reduction in income. Property 1's income drops to $3,600, Property 2's to $3,900, and Property 3's to $4,500. The total monthly income becomes $12,000.

With expenses still at $11,500, Kevin's cash flow is reduced to $500. While this is minimal, it still covers expenses, demonstrating the importance of maintaining strong initial DSCR ratios and conservative underwriting.

Kevin also considers his reserves. He has $60,000 in liquid funds, which covers more than five months of total portfolio expenses. This provides a buffer that allows him to manage temporary declines in income without financial stress.

Through this analysis, Kevin gains confidence in the stability of his portfolio. He identifies that his conservative approach to DSCR and reserves has created a resilient investment structure. He also recognizes the importance of continuing to monitor performance and maintain adequate reserves as he scales. This example illustrates how risk management and stress testing can provide valuable insights into the strength of your portfolio. By understanding how your investments perform under different conditions, you can make informed decisions and build a strategy that supports long-term success.

Chapter 8

Exit Strategies, Refinancing, and Equity Optimization for Airbnb Investors

As you build and scale your Airbnb portfolio using no-income verification loans, one of the most important elements of long-term success is not just how you acquire properties—but how you exit, reposition, and recycle your capital. Many investors focus heavily on acquisition and cash flow, but the true acceleration of wealth comes from understanding how to extract equity, reposition assets, and strategically redeploy capital into new opportunities. This is where exit strategies and refinancing become essential tools, not just optional considerations.

The first concept to understand is that every property should be acquired with an exit strategy in mind. Even if your intention is to hold a property long-term, you should still evaluate how that property could be refinanced, sold, or repositioned in the future. This forward-thinking approach allows you to structure your initial deal in a way that maximizes flexibility and preserves optionality. For example, maintaining a strong DSCR ratio and conservative leverage at acquisition can position you for a future cash-out refinance, enabling you to access equity without selling the property.

Refinancing is one of the most powerful tools available to Airbnb investors. It allows you to replace your existing loan with a new one, often with different terms, and potentially access the equity that has built up in the property. This equity can come from appreciation, loan paydown, or increased property income. In the context of no-income verification loans, refinancing can often be done using DSCR-based programs, meaning you can continue to qualify based on property performance rather than personal income.

There are two primary types of refinancing strategies that Airbnb investors use: rate-and-term refinancing and cash-out refinancing. Rate-and-term refinancing focuses on improving the loan terms, such as securing a lower interest rate or extending the loan term to reduce monthly payments. This can improve cash flow and stability. Cash-out refinancing, on the other hand, allows you to access a portion of the property's equity in the form of cash, which can then be used to fund additional investments.

Cash-out refinancing is a key component of scaling strategies such as BRRRR (Buy, Rehab, Rent, Refinance, Repeat). In the Airbnb context, this strategy involves acquiring a property, optimizing its performance through improvements and management, and then refinancing based on its increased value and income. The capital extracted from the refinance is then used to acquire additional properties, creating a cycle of growth that can significantly accelerate portfolio expansion.

One of the most important factors in refinancing is understanding loan-to-value (LTV) limits. Most lenders will allow cash-out refinancing up to a certain percentage of the property's appraised value, often around 70% to 75% for investment properties. This means that even if your property has appreciated significantly, you may only be able to access a portion of that equity. Planning for this limitation is essential when structuring your deals and evaluating potential returns.

Another critical consideration is the timing of your refinance. Refinancing too early may limit the amount of equity you can access, while waiting too long may expose you to changes in market conditions or interest rates. The ideal timing often depends on a combination of factors, including property performance, market appreciation, and loan seasoning requirements. Many lenders require a certain period—such as six to twelve months—before allowing a refinance, particularly for cash-out transactions.

Property performance plays a central role in refinancing decisions, especially when using DSCR loans. As your Airbnb property generates consistent income and establishes a performance history, it becomes more attractive to lenders.

This can lead to better loan terms, higher appraised values, and increased borrowing capacity. By actively managing and optimizing your property's performance, you not only improve cash flow but also enhance your ability to leverage that property for future growth.

Another important aspect of equity optimization is understanding how improvements and upgrades impact property value. Strategic renovations, enhanced amenities, and improved guest experiences can increase both the income potential and the appraised value of your property. This creates a dual benefit: higher cash flow and increased equity. When executed correctly, these improvements can significantly enhance your return on investment and provide additional leverage for refinancing.

Selling is another exit strategy that should be considered as part of your overall plan. While many investors prefer to hold properties for long-term cash flow, there may be situations where selling is the most advantageous option. This could include taking advantage of strong market conditions, reallocating capital to higher-performing opportunities, or reducing exposure in a particular market. Understanding when and how to sell is an important part of managing your portfolio effectively. Tax considerations also play a role in exit strategies. While this book does not provide tax advice, it is important to be aware that selling a property may trigger capital gains taxes, while refinancing generally does not. This makes refinancing an attractive option for accessing equity without immediate tax consequences. However, each investor's situation is unique, and it is important to consult with professionals to understand the implications of different strategies.

Another advanced strategy involves combining multiple exit approaches. For example, you may refinance a property to extract equity while continuing to hold it for cash flow. Alternatively, you may sell one property to fund the acquisition of several others. The key is to remain flexible and evaluate each decision in the context of your broader portfolio and long-term goals.

Portfolio-level thinking is essential when implementing exit strategies. Instead of evaluating each property in isolation, you should consider how each decision impacts your overall financial position. This includes balancing cash flow, equity, and risk across your portfolio. By taking a holistic approach, you can make more informed decisions and create a portfolio that is both profitable and resilient.

Market conditions also influence exit strategy decisions. Interest rates, property values, and rental demand can all impact the effectiveness of refinancing or selling. Staying informed about these trends allows you to act strategically rather than reactively. For example, refinancing during a period of lower interest rates can improve cash flow, while selling during a strong market can maximize returns.

Ultimately, exit strategies and equity optimization are about control. They allow you to actively manage your investments, access capital, and adapt to changing conditions. By understanding how to use these tools effectively, you can accelerate your growth, improve your returns, and build a portfolio that continues to evolve over time.

The investors who succeed at the highest level are those who think beyond the initial acquisition. They understand that each property is not just an asset, but a source of leverage that can be used to create additional opportunities. By mastering the principles in this chapter, you will be able to unlock that leverage and take your Airbnb investing strategy to the next level.

Real-Life Math Example: Cash-Out Refinance and Equity Recycling Strategy

Consider an investor named Sophia who purchases an Airbnb property for $550,000 using a DSCR loan. She puts down 25%, or $137,500, resulting in a loan amount of $412,500. Her interest rate is 7.5%, and her total monthly expense, including taxes and insurance, is $3,400. The property generates an average monthly income of $5,200, resulting in a DSCR of approximately 1.53 and a monthly cash flow of $1,800. Over the next 12 months, Sophia improves the property by upgrading furnishings, enhancing the listing, and optimizing pricing. As a result, her monthly income increases to $6,000, and the property's performance history strengthens.

During this time, the property also appreciates in value by 10%, increasing its market value to $605,000. Sophia decides to pursue a cash-out refinance. The lender allows up to 75% loan-to-value, meaning she can refinance up to $453,750.

After paying off her existing loan balance, which has been reduced slightly through payments to approximately $405,000, Sophia is able to extract around $48,750 in cash. This capital is tax-free under most circumstances and can be used for new investments.

Sophia combines this $48,750 with additional savings to fund the down payment on a second Airbnb property priced at $500,000. She follows a similar strategy, putting down 25% and securing a DSCR loan. The second property generates $4,800 per month in income with expenses of $3,200, resulting in a DSCR of 1.50 and a monthly cash flow of $1,600.

Now with two properties, Sophia's total monthly cash flow increases to $3,400. Over time, she plans to repeat this process—optimizing performance, refinancing, and reinvesting—to continue growing her portfolio.

This example demonstrates how equity can be transformed into a powerful growth engine. By leveraging refinancing and maintaining strong property performance, Sophia is able to access capital, acquire additional properties, and increase her overall income. This cycle of equity recycling is one of the most effective strategies for scaling an Airbnb portfolio using no-income verification loans.

Chapter 9

Building a Repeatable Airbnb Acquisition System Using No-Income Verification Loans

At this point, you understand how to qualify, structure deals, manage risk, scale, and extract equity. Now comes the most important transformation: turning all of this knowledge into a repeatable system. A system is what separates one-time success from long-term dominance. Without a system, every deal feels like starting over. With a system, each deal becomes faster, easier, and more predictable. This chapter is about building that system—one that allows you to consistently identify, analyze, finance, and acquire profitable Airbnb properties using no-income verification strategies.

The first step in building a repeatable acquisition system is defining your buy box. Your buy box is a clear set of criteria that determines which properties you will pursue and which you will ignore. This includes factors such as location, price range, property type, minimum DSCR, target cash flow, and risk tolerance. By defining these parameters, you eliminate guesswork and focus your efforts only on opportunities that align with your goals. This not only saves time but also increases the quality of your decisions.

Market selection is a critical component of your system. Not all markets are equally suited for Airbnb investing, and choosing the right locations can significantly impact your results. Key factors to consider include tourism demand, local regulations, seasonality, and competition. Markets with strong and consistent demand, favorable regulations, and limited competition are ideal for building a stable and profitable portfolio. By narrowing your focus to a few high-performing markets, you can develop deeper expertise and identify opportunities more efficiently.

Once you have defined your market and buy box, the next step is deal sourcing. This involves identifying potential properties that meet your criteria. Sources can include traditional listings, off-market opportunities, and direct outreach. The goal is to create a consistent pipeline of deals so that you always have opportunities to evaluate. Successful investors treat deal sourcing as an ongoing process rather than a one-time activity.

Deal analysis is where your system begins to take shape. For each potential property, you should evaluate key metrics such as purchase price, projected income, expenses, DSCR, and cash flow. This process should be standardized so that you can quickly and accurately assess whether a deal meets your criteria. By using consistent assumptions and methods, you create a reliable framework for decision-making. Over time, this allows you to evaluate deals more efficiently and with greater confidence.

Financing is the next step in the system, and this is where no-income verification strategies play a central role. By leveraging DSCR loans and other flexible financing options, you can qualify based on property performance rather than personal income. This allows you to move quickly and scale more effectively. Building relationships with lenders and understanding their criteria is essential for ensuring that your deals align with available financing options.

Another important element of your system is pre-qualification. Before actively pursuing deals, you should have a clear understanding of your borrowing capacity, credit profile, and available reserves. This allows you to act quickly when opportunities arise and reduces the risk of delays during the approval process. Pre-qualification also enhances your credibility with sellers and agents, making you a more competitive buyer.

Offer strategy is another key component of your system. This includes determining how to structure your offers, negotiate terms, and position yourself as a strong buyer. Factors such as price, contingencies, and closing timelines all play a role in whether your offer is accepted. By developing a consistent approach to making offers, you increase your chances of securing properties while maintaining favorable terms.

Once a deal is under contract, your system should include a clear process for due diligence and closing. This involves verifying property condition, confirming rental projections, and ensuring that all financing requirements are met. Having a structured approach to this phase reduces the risk of unexpected issues and ensures a smooth transaction.

After closing, your system should transition into optimization and management. This includes setting up your Airbnb listing, implementing pricing strategies, and establishing operational processes. The goal is to maximize property performance as quickly as possible, which not only increases cash flow but also strengthens your position for future financing and scaling.

One of the most powerful aspects of a repeatable system is its ability to compound results. Each successful deal builds on the previous one, increasing your experience, capital, and confidence. As your system becomes more refined, you are able to move faster, make better decisions, and capture more opportunities. This creates a momentum that drives long-term growth. Automation and technology can further enhance your system. Tools for market analysis, pricing optimization, and property management can streamline your operations and reduce manual effort. By leveraging these tools, you can manage a larger portfolio with greater efficiency and consistency.

Another important aspect of building a system is tracking performance. By monitoring key metrics such as occupancy, average daily rate, expenses, and cash flow, you gain valuable insights into what is working and what needs improvement. This data-driven approach allows you to refine your strategy over time and continuously improve your results.

Consistency is the foundation of any successful system. This means following your process even when it is tempting to deviate. While flexibility is important, maintaining discipline ensures that your decisions are based on strategy rather than emotion. This is particularly important in competitive markets, where pressure to act quickly can lead to poor decisions.

As your system evolves, you may also incorporate team members or partners to support your growth. This could include real estate agents, property managers, cleaners, and contractors. Building a reliable team allows you to focus on high-level strategy while ensuring that your operations run smoothly. Ultimately, a repeatable acquisition system is about creating efficiency and predictability. It allows you to approach each deal with confidence, knowing that you have a proven process in place. This reduces stress, increases success rates, and enables you to scale your Airbnb portfolio more effectively.

By mastering the principles in this chapter, you will be able to transform your investing approach from reactive to proactive. Instead of chasing deals, you will create a system that consistently generates opportunities and converts them into profitable investments. This is the key to building a sustainable and scalable Airbnb business using no-income verification loans.

Real-Life Math Example: Building a Repeatable Airbnb Acquisition System

Consider an investor named Ryan who has developed a repeatable system for acquiring Airbnb properties. His buy box includes properties priced between $400,000 and $600,000 in high-demand vacation markets, with a target DSCR of at least 1.25 and a minimum monthly cash flow of $1,200.

Ryan identifies a property listed at $480,000. He plans to put down 25%, or $120,000, resulting in a loan amount of

$360,000. At an interest rate of 7.5%, his monthly principal and interest payment is approximately $2,520. Including taxes and insurance, his total monthly expense is $3,000. Using his standardized analysis process, Ryan estimates an average daily rate of $210 and an occupancy rate of 70%. At full occupancy, the property would generate $6,300 per month. Applying the occupancy rate, the projected monthly income is $4,410.

Ryan calculates the DSCR by dividing $4,410 by $3,000, resulting in a ratio of 1.47, which exceeds his target of 1.25. He also calculates his projected cash flow as $1,410 per month, exceeding his minimum requirement.

Because the property meets his criteria, Ryan proceeds with an offer. He repeats this process for multiple properties, ultimately acquiring three properties within a year. Each property generates similar performance, resulting in a combined monthly cash flow of approximately $4,200.

Ryan tracks his performance data and identifies opportunities to improve. By optimizing pricing and increasing occupancy to 75%, he raises his average monthly income per property to $4,725. This increases his cash flow and strengthens his DSCR ratios, positioning him for future acquisitions.

By following his system consistently, Ryan is able to scale his portfolio efficiently. Each step—from market selection to deal analysis to financing—is standardized, allowing him to move quickly and confidently. Over time, this system becomes a powerful engine for growth, enabling him to build a portfolio of high-performing Airbnb properties without relying on traditional income verification.

Chapter 10

Advanced Airbnb Mortgage Loan Structuring—Combining DSCR, Asset-Based, and Creative Financing to Close Any Deal

At the highest level of Airbnb investing, success is no longer determined by whether you can qualify for a loan—it is determined by how creatively and effectively you can structure financing to close deals that others cannot. This is where advanced loan structuring becomes a true competitive advantage. By combining DSCR loans, asset-based lending, and creative financing strategies, you gain the ability to adapt to virtually any scenario and unlock opportunities that would otherwise be inaccessible.

The first concept to understand is that no single loan product is designed to solve every situation. Each financing option has strengths and limitations, and advanced investors learn how to layer these options together to create customized solutions. DSCR loans provide scalability and simplicity by focusing on property income. Asset-based loans leverage your financial resources, such as cash, investments, or retirement accounts, to support qualification. Creative financing techniques—such as seller financing, subject-to transactions, or private lending—introduce additional flexibility. When combined strategically, these tools allow you to structure deals that meet both lender requirements and your investment goals.

DSCR loans remain the foundation of most advanced Airbnb financing strategies. Their ability to qualify based on property performance makes them ideal for scaling. However, there are situations where a property may not fully meet DSCR requirements, or where additional flexibility is needed. In these cases, asset-based lending can provide a valuable supplement. Asset-based loans evaluate your ability to repay based on your overall financial position rather than income, allowing you to leverage your assets to secure financing.

For example, if a property has strong long-term potential but slightly lower initial DSCR, an asset-based approach may allow you to qualify by demonstrating sufficient liquidity and reserves. This creates an opportunity to acquire the property, improve its performance, and later transition to a DSCR loan through refinancing. This type of strategic sequencing is a hallmark of advanced investors, who view financing as a dynamic process rather than a one-time event.

Creative financing adds another layer of flexibility. Seller financing, for instance, allows you to negotiate terms directly with the property owner, potentially reducing the need for traditional financing altogether. This can include lower down payments, flexible interest rates, or deferred payments. Subject-to transactions involve taking over an existing mortgage, which can be advantageous if the current loan has favorable terms. Private lending introduces additional capital sources that can be used to bridge gaps or fund acquisitions quickly.

One of the key advantages of combining these strategies is the ability to overcome limitations. For example, if a DSCR loan requires a higher down payment than you are comfortable with, you might use private capital to supplement your funds. If a property does not initially meet DSCR requirements, you might use a short-term creative financing solution to acquire it, improve its performance, and then refinance into a DSCR loan. This flexibility allows you to adapt to different situations and maintain momentum in your investing journey.

Another important aspect of advanced structuring is understanding how to sequence your financing. This means planning not just how you will acquire a property, but how you will transition it over time. For example, you might start with a short-term loan or creative financing arrangement, stabilize the property's income, and then refinance into a long-term DSCR loan. This approach allows you to optimize both acquisition and long-term performance.

Leverage becomes even more powerful when used in combination with these strategies. By layering different financing options, you can reduce your initial capital requirements and increase your return on investment. However, this also requires careful risk management. Each layer of financing introduces additional complexity, and it is important to ensure that your overall structure remains stable and sustainable. This includes maintaining strong reserves, conservative projections, and clear exit strategies.

Another advanced concept is the use of cross-collateralization. This involves using multiple properties or assets to secure a single loan, increasing your borrowing capacity. While this can be a powerful tool, it also introduces additional risk, as multiple assets may be tied to a single obligation. Understanding when and how to use this strategy is essential for maintaining control over your portfolio.

Portfolio-level structuring is also an important consideration. As your portfolio grows, you may begin to structure financing across multiple properties rather than on an individual basis. This can include blanket loans, portfolio loans, or other arrangements that provide greater flexibility and efficiency. These structures can simplify management and create new opportunities for scaling, but they also require a deeper understanding of lender requirements and risk management.

Negotiation plays a significant role in advanced structuring. This includes negotiating not only purchase terms but also financing terms. Building relationships with lenders, private investors, and other stakeholders can provide access to more flexible options and better terms. Experienced investors understand that every deal is negotiable, and they use this to their advantage to create win-win scenarios.

Another key element is adaptability. The real estate market is constantly evolving, and the ability to adjust your strategy is critical. Interest rates, lending guidelines, and market conditions can all change, and advanced investors stay informed and flexible. By understanding multiple financing options and how they can be combined, you are better equipped to navigate these changes and continue moving forward.

Risk management remains a central theme in advanced structuring. While creative strategies can unlock opportunities, they also require a disciplined approach. This includes thoroughly analyzing each deal, understanding the terms of each financing component, and ensuring that your overall structure is sustainable. By maintaining a balance between creativity and caution, you can maximize opportunities while minimizing risk.

Another important consideration is scalability. Advanced structuring should not only help you close individual deals but also support your long-term growth. This means selecting strategies that can be repeated and adapted as your portfolio expands. By building a framework that integrates multiple financing options, you create a system that can evolve with your business.

Ultimately, advanced Airbnb mortgage loan structuring is about control and flexibility. It allows you to move beyond the limitations of any single financing method and create customized solutions that align with your goals. This level of sophistication is what enables experienced investors to consistently close deals, even in challenging markets.

By mastering the principles in this chapter, you will be able to approach each deal with a broader perspective and a deeper toolkit. You will understand how to combine DSCR, asset-based, and creative financing strategies to overcome obstacles and unlock opportunities. This is the final step in transforming your investing approach into a highly adaptable and scalable system.

Real-Life Math Example: Combining DSCR, Asset-Based, and Creative Financing

Consider an investor named Ethan who identifies a high-potential Airbnb property priced at $800,000. The property has strong long-term potential but currently generates income that results in a DSCR of only 1.10, below the lender's minimum requirement of 1.20. Ethan decides to use a combination of financing strategies to structure the deal.

First, Ethan negotiates seller financing for 10% of the purchase price, or $80,000. This reduces the amount he needs to finance through a traditional lender. He then applies for a DSCR loan covering 65% of the purchase price, or $520,000. This results in a monthly principal and interest payment of approximately $3,900. Including taxes and insurance, the total monthly expense is $4,800.

The remaining 25%, or $200,000, is covered through a combination of Ethan's own funds and a private loan. This layered approach allows him to close the deal despite the initial DSCR shortfall.

The property currently generates $5,280 per month in income, resulting in a DSCR of 1.10. Ethan implements improvements, including upgraded furnishings and optimized pricing, increasing the average daily rate and occupancy. Within six months, the property's monthly income rises to $6,240.

With the improved income, the DSCR increases to approximately 1.30 ($6,240 divided by $4,800), making the property eligible for refinancing under standard DSCR guidelines. Ethan refinances the property, consolidating his financing into a single DSCR loan at 75% loan-to-value, or $600,000.

After paying off the original DSCR loan, seller financing, and private loan, Ethan is able to simplify his financing structure and potentially extract additional equity. His monthly expense remains manageable, and his improved income results in a cash flow of approximately $1,440 per month.

This example demonstrates how combining multiple financing strategies can allow you to acquire and stabilize a property that would not qualify under a single loan type. By understanding how to layer DSCR, asset-based, and creative financing, Ethan is able to close the deal, improve performance, and transition to a more efficient long-term structure.

Chapter 11

Building a Long-Term Airbnb Wealth Plan Using No-Income Verification Strategies

As you reach this stage, you are no longer just learning how to get approved for Airbnb mortgage loans—you are learning how to build a long-term wealth system. Everything you have covered so far—DSCR loans, bank statement options, credit positioning, reserves, deal structuring, scaling, refinancing, and advanced financing—now comes together into one unified objective: creating sustainable, long-term financial freedom through a strategically built Airbnb portfolio.

The first and most important shift at this level is moving from a transaction mindset to a portfolio mindset. A transaction mindset focuses on individual deals—buying a property, getting approved, and generating cash flow. A portfolio mindset focuses on how each property contributes to your overall financial ecosystem. This includes balancing cash flow, equity growth, risk exposure, and scalability. When you think in terms of a portfolio, every decision becomes more strategic and aligned with long-term goals. The foundation of a long-term Airbnb wealth plan is consistent cash flow. Cash flow provides the financial fuel that supports your lifestyle, builds reserves, and funds future investments. Unlike appreciation, which is influenced by market conditions, cash flow is something you can actively manage and optimize. By selecting high-performing properties, implementing effective management strategies, and maintaining strong DSCR ratios, you create a reliable income stream that grows over time.

However, cash flow is only one part of the equation. Equity growth is equally important. As your properties appreciate in value and your loan balances decrease, your equity increases. This equity represents stored wealth that can be accessed through refinancing or leveraged for additional investments. Understanding how to balance cash flow and equity growth is essential for building a portfolio that is both profitable and scalable.

Another key component of long-term wealth planning is capital recycling. As discussed in previous chapters, refinancing allows you to extract equity and reinvest it into new properties. This creates a cycle of growth where each property contributes to the acquisition of the next. Over time, this compounding effect can significantly accelerate your portfolio expansion. The key is to execute this strategy in a disciplined manner, ensuring that each step strengthens your overall financial position. Risk management remains a central theme in long-term planning. As your portfolio grows, so does your exposure to market fluctuations, operational challenges, and financial risks. Maintaining strong reserves, diversifying your investments, and using conservative underwriting assumptions are essential for protecting your portfolio. Long-term wealth is not just about growth—it is about preserving and stabilizing that growth over time.

Another important consideration is lifestyle alignment. Your Airbnb portfolio should support your desired lifestyle, not create unnecessary stress or complexity. This means building systems and processes that allow you to manage your properties efficiently, whether through automation, delegation, or professional management. By aligning your investments with your lifestyle goals, you create a business that is both profitable and sustainable.

Tax strategy is another factor that plays a role in long-term wealth planning. While specific strategies will vary, it is important to understand that real estate offers unique tax advantages, including depreciation and potential deferral of capital gains through certain transactions. Integrating these considerations into your overall plan can enhance your returns and improve your financial efficiency. Financing strategy also evolves as you build a long-term plan. While DSCR loans may be the primary tool for acquisition and scaling, you may incorporate other financing options as your portfolio grows. This could include portfolio loans, asset-based lending, or even partnerships. The goal is to create a flexible financing framework that supports your growth while maintaining stability.

Another advanced concept in long-term planning is the idea of portfolio optimization. This involves periodically evaluating your properties to determine whether they are performing at their highest potential. This may include refinancing, selling underperforming assets, or reallocating capital to more profitable opportunities. By actively managing your portfolio, you ensure that it continues to align with your goals and market conditions.

Time is one of the most powerful factors in building wealth. Real estate investing is not just about short-term gains—it is about long-term accumulation and compounding. As your properties generate income, appreciate in value, and contribute to your overall financial position, the cumulative effect becomes significant. Understanding and leveraging this time factor is essential for achieving lasting success.

Another important aspect of long-term planning is adaptability. Markets change, regulations evolve, and new opportunities emerge. The ability to adjust your strategy while maintaining a clear vision is critical. This includes staying informed, continuously learning, and being willing to pivot when necessary. Flexibility allows you to navigate challenges and capitalize on new opportunities as they arise.

Building a long-term Airbnb wealth plan also involves setting clear goals. These goals may include a target number of properties, a specific level of monthly cash flow, or a desired net worth. By defining your objectives, you create a roadmap that guides your decisions and keeps you focused. Regularly reviewing and adjusting these goals ensures that you remain aligned with your vision.

Another key element is discipline. Success in real estate investing requires consistent execution of proven strategies. This includes following your acquisition criteria, maintaining strong financial practices, and avoiding impulsive decisions. Discipline ensures that your actions are aligned with your long-term plan, even in the face of short-term challenges.

As your portfolio grows, you may also consider legacy planning. This involves thinking about how your investments will be managed and transferred in the future. Whether your goal is to create generational wealth, provide financial security for your family, or build a lasting business, planning ahead ensures that your efforts have a lasting impact. Ultimately, building a long-term Airbnb wealth plan is about creating a system that works for you. It is about aligning your investments with your goals, managing risk effectively, and leveraging opportunities for growth. By integrating all the strategies you have learned, you can create a portfolio that generates consistent income, builds equity, and supports your financial independence.

This chapter represents the culmination of your journey through no-income verification Airbnb mortgage lending. You now have the knowledge and tools to not only acquire properties but to build a sustainable and scalable business. The next step is to apply these principles consistently and continue refining your approach as you grow.

Real-Life Math Example: Building a Long-Term Airbnb Wealth Plan

Consider an investor named Maria who sets a goal of building a portfolio that generates $10,000 per month in net cash flow within five years. She begins by acquiring her first Airbnb property for $500,000 using a DSCR loan with a 25% down payment of $125,000. The property generates $4,800 per month in income with expenses of $3,200, resulting in a monthly cash flow of $1,600. In the first year, Maria accumulates $19,200 in cash flow and observes a 5% increase in property value, bringing it to $525,000. She refinances the property at 75% loan-to-value, extracting approximately $30,000 in equity. She combines this with savings to acquire a second property for $550,000.

The second property generates $5,200 per month in income with expenses of $3,600, resulting in a cash flow of $1,600. With two properties, Maria's total monthly cash flow increases to $3,200.

Over the next two years, Maria repeats this process, acquiring two additional properties with similar performance. By year three, she owns four properties generating a combined monthly cash flow of $6,400.

In years four and five, Maria continues to optimize her properties, increasing average daily rates and occupancy. Her average monthly cash flow per property rises to $2,000. With five properties, her total monthly cash flow reaches $10,000, achieving her goal.

In addition to cash flow, Maria's properties have appreciated in value, increasing her overall equity. By strategically refinancing and reinvesting, she has built a portfolio that generates consistent income and continues to grow in value.

This example illustrates how a long-term wealth plan can be executed through consistent application of no-income verification strategies. By focusing on both cash flow and equity growth, Maria is able to achieve financial independence and create a sustainable investment portfolio.

Chapter 12

Final Blueprint—From First Deal to Financial Freedom with Airbnb No-Income Verification Loans

At this point, you have everything you need. You understand how Airbnb mortgage loans work without traditional income verification, how to structure deals, how to optimize credit and reserves, how to scale, how to manage risk, how to refinance and extract equity, and how to build a repeatable acquisition system. Now it is time to bring it all together into one complete blueprint—a step-by-step framework that takes you from your first deal to long-term financial freedom.

The first stage of the blueprint is foundation building. This is where you prepare yourself as a borrower and investor before acquiring your first property. It includes optimizing your credit, building reserves, understanding DSCR requirements, and identifying your target markets. This stage is critical because it sets the tone for everything that follows. A strong foundation allows you to move quickly and confidently when opportunities arise.

The second stage is your first acquisition. This is where theory becomes practice. Your goal is not to find the perfect deal, but to find a strong, well-structured deal that meets DSCR requirements and generates positive cash flow. This first property serves as both an income-producing asset and a learning experience. It teaches you how to analyze deals, work with lenders, and manage an Airbnb property effectively.

Once your first property is stabilized, you move into the optimization stage. This involves improving the property's performance through better pricing strategies, enhanced guest experience, and operational efficiency. The goal is to maximize income and strengthen your DSCR ratio. This not only increases your cash flow but also positions you for future refinancing and scaling opportunities.

The fourth stage is expansion. Using the knowledge and experience gained from your first property, you begin acquiring additional properties. This is where no-income verification loans truly shine, allowing you to qualify based on each property's performance rather than your personal income. By repeating the acquisition and optimization process, you begin to build a portfolio of income-producing assets.

As your portfolio grows, you enter the scaling stage. This involves refining your systems, improving efficiency, and leveraging financing strategies to accelerate growth. You may begin to use refinancing to extract equity, allowing you to fund additional acquisitions without relying solely on savings. At this stage, your focus shifts from individual deals to portfolio-level performance.

The next stage is stabilization. This is where you focus on maintaining consistent performance across your portfolio. This includes managing risk, maintaining reserves, and ensuring that each property continues to meet your performance criteria. Stabilization is essential for long-term success, as it ensures that your growth is sustainable and not overly reliant on favorable market conditions.

The seventh stage is optimization at the portfolio level. This involves evaluating your properties collectively and making strategic decisions to improve overall performance. This may include refinancing, selling underperforming assets, or reallocating capital to higher-performing opportunities. By actively managing your portfolio, you ensure that it continues to align with your goals.

The final stage is financial freedom. This is the point where your portfolio generates sufficient income to cover your expenses and support your desired lifestyle. At this stage, you have the flexibility to choose how you spend your time, whether that involves continuing to grow your portfolio, pursuing other ventures, or simply enjoying the benefits of your investments.

One of the most important aspects of this blueprint is its repeatability. Each stage builds on the previous one, creating a cycle of growth and optimization. By following this framework consistently, you can move from one stage to the next with confidence and clarity. This eliminates uncertainty and allows you to focus on execution.

Another key element is adaptability. While the blueprint provides a structured approach, it is not rigid. You can adjust your strategy based on market conditions, personal goals, and new opportunities. This flexibility ensures that your approach remains relevant and effective over time.

Discipline is also essential. Success in Airbnb investing requires consistent application of the principles you have learned. This includes adhering to your acquisition criteria, maintaining strong financial practices, and managing risk effectively. Discipline ensures that your actions are aligned with your long-term goals.

Mindset plays a significant role in your success. Building a portfolio takes time, effort, and persistence. There will be challenges and setbacks along the way, but maintaining a long-term perspective allows you to navigate these obstacles and continue moving forward. Confidence in your strategy and commitment to your goals are key to achieving lasting success.

Another important consideration is continuous learning. The real estate market is constantly evolving, and staying informed allows you to adapt and improve. This includes keeping up with market trends, lending guidelines, and new strategies. By continuously refining your approach, you ensure that your blueprint remains effective.

Collaboration can also enhance your success. Working with experienced professionals, such as lenders, real estate agents, and property managers, provides valuable insights and support. Building a strong network allows you to leverage expertise and access opportunities that may not be available otherwise.

Tracking progress is another critical component of the blueprint. By monitoring key metrics such as cash flow, DSCR, and equity growth, you can evaluate your performance and make informed decisions. This data-driven approach allows you to identify areas for improvement and optimize your strategy over time.

As you move through the stages of this blueprint, you will begin to see the compounding effect of your efforts. Each property contributes to your overall income and equity, creating a snowball effect that accelerates your progress. This compounding is one of the most powerful aspects of real estate investing. Ultimately, this blueprint is about creating a system that works for you. It is about aligning your investments with your goals, managing risk effectively, and leveraging opportunities for growth. By following this framework, you can build a portfolio that generates consistent income, builds wealth, and supports your financial independence.

This is not just a strategy—it is a roadmap to a new way of thinking about money, investing, and opportunity. By mastering the principles in this book and applying them consistently, you have the potential to transform your financial future and create a life of freedom and flexibility.

Real-Life Math Example: Full Blueprint from First Deal to Financial Freedom

Consider an investor named Jason who follows this blueprint over a five-year period. In year one, he purchases his first Airbnb property for $450,000 using a DSCR loan with a 25% down payment of $112,500. The property generates $4,200 per month in income with expenses of $2,800, resulting in a cash flow of $1,400.

In year two, Jason optimizes the property, increasing income to $4,800 per month. He refinances the property, extracting

$25,000 in equity, which he uses along with savings to purchase a second property for $500,000. The second property generates $4,600 per month in income with expenses of $3,200, resulting in a cash flow of $1,400.

By the end of year two, Jason's total monthly cash flow is $2,800.

In year three, Jason repeats the process, acquiring a third property for $550,000. This property generates $5,000 per month in income with expenses of $3,500, resulting in a cash flow of $1,500. His total monthly cash flow increases to $4,300.

In year four, Jason acquires a fourth property for $600,000, generating $5,400 per month in income with expenses of $3,800, resulting in a cash flow of $1,600. His total monthly cash flow reaches $5,900.

In year five, Jason focuses on optimization, increasing the average cash flow per property to $2,000 through improved pricing and occupancy. With four properties, his total monthly cash flow reaches $8,000. He then acquires a fifth property, bringing his total monthly cash flow to $10,000.

At this point, Jason has achieved financial freedom, with his portfolio generating sufficient income to cover his expenses. In addition, his properties have appreciated in value, increasing his overall equity and net worth.

This example demonstrates how the blueprint can be applied in practice. By following a structured approach and consistently applying the strategies outlined in this book, Jason is able to build a portfolio that generates income, builds wealth, and supports his long-term goals.

Chapter 13

Becoming the Bank—Advanced Capital Control and Infinite Scaling Strategies for Airbnb Investors

At the highest level of Airbnb investing, there is one final evolution that separates top-tier investors from everyone else: they stop relying solely on banks—and begin to think like one. This chapter is about that transformation. It is about moving from borrower to capital controller, from deal participant to deal orchestrator. When you reach this level, financing is no longer a limitation. It becomes a tool you design, control, and deploy to scale faster than traditional investors ever could.

The first concept to understand is that banks do not make money by owning assets—they make money by controlling capital. They lend money, collect interest, and use leverage to multiply returns. As an Airbnb investor, you can apply the same principles on a smaller scale. Instead of only using your own capital, you begin to use other people's money strategically, structuring deals in a way that benefits both you and your capital sources.

This shift begins with understanding capital sources. These can include private lenders, business lines of credit, HELOCs, partnerships, and even investor pools. Each source has its own cost, flexibility, and requirements. The key is to match the right source of capital to the right opportunity. For example, a private lender may provide fast funding for a time-sensitive deal, while a DSCR loan may provide long-term stability once the property is stabilized.

One of the most powerful strategies at this level is capital stacking. Capital stacking involves combining multiple sources of funding to complete a deal. For example, you might use a DSCR loan for the primary financing, a private lender for the down payment, and your own reserves for closing costs. This layered approach allows you to control larger assets with less of your own capital, increasing your return on investment and accelerating your ability to scale.

Another key concept is yield arbitrage. This is the difference between the cost of your capital and the return generated by your investments. For example, if you borrow money at 8% and invest it in a property that generates a 15% return, you are capturing the spread between those two rates. This is how banks generate profit, and it is a principle you can apply to your Airbnb portfolio. The goal is to consistently acquire assets that produce returns higher than your cost of capital. To operate at this level, you must also develop strong deal presentation skills. When using other people's money, you are no longer just analyzing deals for yourself—you are presenting opportunities to potential partners or lenders. This requires clear, data-driven analysis that demonstrates the strength of the investment. Metrics such as DSCR, cash flow, occupancy, and market trends become essential components of your pitch.

Risk management becomes even more critical when working with external capital. You are not only responsible for your own financial outcomes, but also for the expectations of your partners or lenders. This means maintaining conservative assumptions, strong reserves, and clear exit strategies. By managing risk effectively, you build trust and create the foundation for long-term relationships.

Another advanced strategy is creating your own lending ecosystem. As your portfolio grows and your cash flow increases, you may begin to lend money to other investors. This allows you to earn interest on your capital while maintaining exposure to real estate opportunities. Over time, this can evolve into a hybrid model where you both invest in properties and act as a capital provider, further diversifying your income streams.

Business credit also plays a significant role in becoming the bank. By building strong business credit profiles, you can access lines of credit and funding that are separate from your personal finances. This increases your borrowing capacity and provides additional flexibility in structuring deals. Strategic use of business credit can support acquisitions, renovations, and operational expenses, allowing you to scale more efficiently.

Another important element is velocity of money. This refers to how quickly you can deploy and redeploy capital. The faster your capital moves, the more opportunities you can capture. This is why strategies such as refinancing and equity extraction are so powerful—they allow you to recycle capital and use it multiple times. By increasing the velocity of your money, you accelerate your overall growth.

Partnerships become a valuable tool at this stage. By partnering with others, you can combine resources, expertise, and capital to pursue larger opportunities. This might involve joint ventures, equity partnerships, or syndications. The key is to structure these partnerships in a way that aligns incentives and creates mutual benefit. Clear communication and well-defined roles are essential for success.

Another advanced concept is control versus ownership. Many investors focus on owning properties outright, but at this level, control is often more important than ownership. By structuring deals creatively, you can control assets with a smaller equity stake, allowing you to diversify and scale more effectively. This approach maximizes your leverage and expands your reach.

Systems and automation become increasingly important as you scale. Managing multiple properties, capital sources, and partnerships requires efficient processes. By building systems for deal analysis, financing, and operations, you can maintain consistency and reduce complexity. This allows you to focus on high-level strategy while ensuring that your business runs smoothly.

Market awareness is also critical. As you operate at a higher level, you must stay informed about changes in lending, real estate markets, and economic conditions. This allows you to adjust your strategy and capitalize on new opportunities. Being proactive rather than reactive is a key trait of successful investors.

Ultimately, becoming the bank is about mindset. It is about seeing yourself not just as an investor, but as a capital strategist. It is about understanding how money flows, how deals are structured, and how value is created. This perspective allows you to operate with a level of confidence and control that sets you apart from others.

By mastering the principles in this chapter, you move beyond traditional investing and enter a new phase of growth. You gain the ability to structure deals creatively, leverage multiple sources of capital, and scale your Airbnb portfolio in a way that is both efficient and sustainable. This is the final level of mastery in no-income verification Airbnb investing.

Real-Life Math Example: Capital Stacking and Yield Arbitrage in Action

Consider an investor named Chris who identifies an Airbnb property priced at $900,000 with strong income potential. The property is projected to generate $8,100 per month in income, with total expenses of $5,400, resulting in a monthly cash flow of $2,700.

Chris structures the deal using capital stacking. He secures a DSCR loan for 70% of the purchase price, or $630,000. The monthly payment on this loan, including taxes and insurance, is $4,800. He then uses a private lender to fund 20% of the purchase price, or $180,000, at an interest rate of 10%, resulting in a monthly payment of $1,500. Chris contributes the remaining 10%, or $90,000, from his own funds.

The total monthly expense, including both loans and property costs, is $6,300. With a monthly income of $8,100, the property generates a net cash flow of $1,800.

Chris analyzes the yield arbitrage in this deal. His blended cost of capital is calculated by combining the interest rates of the DSCR loan and the private loan. The DSCR loan at 7.5% on $630,000 and the private loan at 10% on $180,000 result in an average cost of capital of approximately 8.2%.

The property generates an annual cash flow of $21,600 ($1,800 multiplied by 12). In addition, the total investment of $90,000 yields a return of 24% annually ($21,600 divided by $90,000). This high return is achieved through leverage and capital stacking.

After one year, Chris improves the property's performance, increasing income to $9,000 per month. He refinances the property, replacing both loans with a single DSCR loan at 75% loan-to-value, or $675,000. This allows him to pay off the private lender and reduce his cost of capital.

With the new loan, his monthly expense drops to $5,200, and his cash flow increases to $3,800 per month. Chris has effectively used capital stacking to acquire the property, improve its performance, and transition to a more efficient financing structure.

This example demonstrates how advanced investors use multiple sources of capital to control larger assets, generate strong returns, and optimize their financing over time. By understanding and applying these principles, Chris is able to scale his Airbnb portfolio while maximizing efficiency and profitability.

Chapter 14

Legacy Wealth, Exit Domination, and Building a Multi-Generational Airbnb Empire

At the highest level of Airbnb investing, the focus shifts once again—this time from building wealth to preserving, multiplying, and transferring it. You are no longer simply acquiring properties or scaling income. You are building an empire. An ecosystem of assets, systems, capital, and strategy designed to last beyond your lifetime. This chapter is about thinking bigger, planning further, and structuring your Airbnb portfolio in a way that creates long-term legacy wealth.

The first shift in this stage is redefining success. Earlier, success may have meant closing your first deal, reaching a certain level of cash flow, or acquiring multiple properties. Now, success is measured by sustainability, durability, and impact. It is about building a portfolio that continues to generate income, grow in value, and provide opportunities for future generations. This requires a different level of thinking—one that prioritizes long-term stability over short-term gains.

A key component of legacy wealth is ownership structure. How you hold your properties can significantly impact your ability to manage, protect, and transfer them. Many investors use entities such as LLCs or holding companies to create layers of protection and organization. As your portfolio grows, you may develop a structure that includes multiple entities, each serving a specific purpose. This not only protects your assets but also simplifies management and creates a framework for expansion.

Another important element is succession planning. This involves determining how your portfolio will be managed and transferred in the future. Whether your goal is to pass your assets to family members, partners, or other beneficiaries, having a clear plan ensures that your legacy is preserved. This includes documenting processes, establishing roles, and creating systems that can operate independently of your direct involvement.

Cash flow remains central, but its purpose evolves. Instead of focusing solely on personal income, cash flow becomes a tool for reinvestment, expansion, and stability. A portion of your cash flow may be used to acquire new properties, while another portion is allocated to reserves and maintenance. This disciplined approach ensures that your portfolio remains strong and continues to grow over time.

Equity also plays a critical role in legacy building. As your properties appreciate and your loan balances decrease, your equity becomes a significant store of wealth. This equity can be leveraged for additional investments, used as collateral for new opportunities, or simply held as long-term value. Understanding how to manage and optimize this equity is essential for building a lasting portfolio.

Another advanced concept at this stage is portfolio consolidation and optimization. As your portfolio grows, you may identify opportunities to restructure or streamline your assets. This could involve refinancing multiple properties into a single portfolio loan, selling underperforming assets, or reallocating capital to higher-performing opportunities. These decisions are not about short-term gains—they are about strengthening the overall structure of your portfolio.

Diversification becomes even more important when building a legacy. This includes diversifying across markets, property types, and even income streams. While Airbnb properties may remain the core of your portfolio, you may also explore complementary investments such as long-term rentals, commercial properties, or lending activities. This diversification reduces risk and creates multiple pathways for income and growth.

Another critical aspect of legacy wealth is control of operations. As your portfolio expands, it becomes increasingly important to build systems that allow your business to operate without constant oversight. This includes standardizing processes, automating tasks, and potentially building a team to manage day-to-day operations. The goal is to create a business that is not dependent on your direct involvement, allowing it to continue functioning and growing over time.

Branding and positioning can also play a role in building a long-term Airbnb empire. As you acquire more properties, you may develop a recognizable brand associated with quality, consistency, and exceptional guest experiences. This brand can enhance your competitive advantage, increase occupancy rates, and create additional opportunities for expansion.

Another advanced strategy is creating a capital engine within your portfolio. This involves using your existing assets to generate additional capital through refinancing, lending, or partnerships. By continuously recycling and deploying capital, you create a self-sustaining system that fuels ongoing growth. This is how portfolios transition from static collections of properties to dynamic wealth-generating machines.

Risk management remains essential, but at this level, it becomes more strategic. You are no longer just protecting individual properties—you are protecting an entire ecosystem. This includes maintaining strong reserves, monitoring market conditions, and ensuring that your portfolio remains balanced and resilient. By taking a proactive approach to risk, you safeguard your long-term wealth.

Another important consideration is adaptability across generations. Markets, technologies, and regulations will continue to evolve, and your portfolio must be able to adapt. This means building systems and strategies that are flexible and can be adjusted over time. It also means educating and preparing those who will manage your assets in the future, ensuring that your legacy continues to grow.

The concept of exit domination is also critical at this stage. This means having the ability to exit any position strategically and on your terms. Whether through refinancing, selling, or restructuring, you maintain control over your assets and your capital. This flexibility allows you to respond to opportunities and challenges effectively, ensuring that your portfolio remains optimized.

Another key element is mindset. Building a multi-generational Airbnb empire requires patience, discipline, and a long-term perspective. It is about making decisions that may not yield immediate results but contribute to lasting success. This mindset allows you to navigate challenges and stay focused on your ultimate goals. As you bring all these elements together, you begin to see the full picture. Your Airbnb portfolio is no longer just a collection of properties—it is a system designed to generate income, build equity, and create opportunities for generations to come. It is a business, a financial engine, and a legacy all in one.

By mastering the principles in this chapter, you position yourself at the highest level of Airbnb investing. You gain the ability to not only build wealth but to sustain and multiply it over time. This is the culmination of your journey—a transformation from investor to architect of a long-term financial empire.

Real-Life Math Example: Building a Multi-Generational Airbnb Portfolio

Consider an investor named Anthony who has built a portfolio of 10 Airbnb properties over several years. Each property was acquired using no-income verification strategies and generates an average monthly income of $5,500 with expenses of $3,800, resulting in a cash flow of $1,700 per property.

Across 10 properties, Anthony's total monthly income is $55,000, with total expenses of $38,000, resulting in a net monthly cash flow of $17,000. Annually, this equates to

$204,000 in cash flow. Over time, the properties have appreciated in value. Each property, originally purchased for an average of $500,000, is now worth $650,000. The total portfolio value is $6.5 million. With average loan balances of $375,000 per property, the total debt is $3.75 million, resulting in total equity of $2.75 million.

Anthony decides to optimize his portfolio by refinancing into a portfolio loan at 70% loan-to-value. This allows him to access approximately $4.55 million in financing. After paying off existing loans, he extracts $800,000 in additional capital.

He uses this capital to acquire four additional properties, each generating $1,800 per month in cash flow. This increases his total monthly cash flow by $7,200, bringing his total to $24,200 per month.

Anthony also allocates a portion of his cash flow to reserves and reinvestment, ensuring that his portfolio remains stable and continues to grow. By building systems and a team to manage operations, he reduces his day-to-day involvement while maintaining performance.

Over time, Anthony's portfolio continues to expand, generating increasing income and equity. By structuring his assets effectively and planning for succession, he creates a system that can be passed on and managed by future generations. This example demonstrates how consistent application of no-income verification strategies, combined with long-term planning and optimization, can lead to the creation of a multi-generational Airbnb empire.

Chapter 15

The Final Execution Plan—Turning Knowledge into Action and Building Your Airbnb Empire Now

You have reached the final stage of this journey, and now everything comes down to one thing: execution. Knowledge without action creates nothing. Strategy without implementation produces no results. At this level, the difference between those who succeed and those who stay stuck is not information—it is the ability to act decisively, consistently, and intelligently. This chapter is your execution plan. It is designed to take everything you have learned and turn it into a clear, actionable path that you can begin immediately.

The first and most important step is eliminating hesitation. Many investors spend months or even years analyzing, planning, and waiting for the perfect moment. The truth is, there is no perfect moment. Markets change, interest rates fluctuate, and opportunities come and go. The only way to move forward is to take action with the best information you have at the time. This does not mean acting recklessly—it means acting strategically and decisively. Your execution plan begins with clarity. You must define exactly what you are trying to achieve. This includes your target number of properties, your desired monthly cash flow, and your timeline. Without clear goals, it is difficult to measure progress or make informed decisions. These goals become your guiding framework, helping you stay focused and aligned as you move forward.

The next step is preparation. Before you begin acquiring properties, you must ensure that your financial profile is ready. This includes optimizing your credit, building reserves, and understanding your borrowing capacity. These elements form the foundation of your execution plan. The stronger your foundation, the easier it will be to secure financing and close deals.

Once your foundation is in place, you move into deal flow creation. This is where you actively begin searching for opportunities that meet your criteria. Your goal is to create a consistent pipeline of potential deals so that you always have options to evaluate. This process should be systematic and ongoing, allowing you to identify opportunities quickly and efficiently.

Deal analysis is the next critical step. For each potential property, you must evaluate its financial viability. This includes calculating projected income, expenses, DSCR, and cash flow. Your analysis should be consistent and based on realistic assumptions. This ensures that you are making informed decisions and avoiding unnecessary risk.

Once you identify a strong deal, the next step is commitment. This is where many investors hesitate. You must be willing to move forward with confidence, knowing that you have done your analysis and that the deal meets your criteria. This does not mean ignoring risks—it means understanding them and deciding that the opportunity outweighs them.

Financing is where your preparation pays off. By leveraging no-income verification loans, you can qualify based on property performance rather than personal income. This allows you to move quickly and take advantage of opportunities. Having relationships with lenders and understanding their requirements is essential for ensuring a smooth process.

Closing the deal is a milestone, but it is not the end—it is the beginning of the next phase. Once you acquire a property, your focus shifts to optimization. This involves setting up the property for maximum performance, including pricing strategies, guest experience, and operational efficiency. The goal is to generate strong income and establish a solid performance history.

As your first property stabilizes, you repeat the process. This is where momentum begins to build. Each successful deal increases your experience, confidence, and financial capacity. Over time, this creates a compounding effect that accelerates your growth.

Consistency is the key to execution. It is not about making one big move—it is about making consistent, strategic moves over time. This includes continuously sourcing deals, analyzing opportunities, and executing your plan. By maintaining this consistency, you create a system that produces results.

Another important aspect of execution is adaptability. While your plan provides a framework, you must be willing to adjust based on market conditions and new information. This includes adapting your strategy, exploring new opportunities, and refining your approach. Flexibility allows you to stay competitive and capitalize on changing conditions.

Time management also plays a critical role. Building an Airbnb portfolio requires focus and discipline. You must prioritize high-impact activities such as deal sourcing, analysis, and financing, while minimizing distractions. This ensures that your efforts are directed toward actions that produce results.

Tracking progress is essential for maintaining momentum. By monitoring key metrics such as cash flow, DSCR, and portfolio growth, you can evaluate your performance and make informed decisions. This data-driven approach allows you to identify areas for improvement and optimize your strategy.

Another key element is resilience. There will be challenges, setbacks, and unexpected obstacles along the way. The ability to stay focused and continue moving forward is what separates successful investors from those who give up. Each challenge is an opportunity to learn and improve.

Building a support system can also enhance your execution. This includes working with lenders, real estate agents, and other professionals who can provide guidance and support. Surrounding yourself with the right people allows you to leverage their expertise and accelerate your progress.

As you execute your plan, you will begin to see results. Your portfolio will grow, your cash flow will increase, and your confidence will strengthen. This is the point where your efforts begin to compound, creating a cycle of growth and opportunity.

Ultimately, execution is about turning potential into reality. It is about taking the knowledge you have gained and applying it in a way that produces tangible results. By following this plan, you can move from learning to doing, from planning to achieving, and from dreaming to building.

This is your moment to act. You have the knowledge, the strategy, and the tools. The only thing left is execution. By committing to this process and taking consistent action, you can build the Airbnb portfolio you envision and achieve the financial freedom you desire.

Real-Life Math Example: Executing the Plan Step by Step

Consider an investor named Marcus who decides to follow this execution plan. His goal is to acquire three Airbnb properties within two years, each generating at least $1,500 per month in cash flow.

Marcus begins by preparing his financial profile. He improves his credit score to 720 and builds $60,000 in reserves. He identifies his target market and begins sourcing deals.

In the first three months, Marcus analyzes multiple properties and identifies one priced at $480,000. He puts down 25%, or $120,000, resulting in a loan amount of $360,000. His monthly expense is $3,000, and the property generates $4,500 per month in income, resulting in a cash flow of $1,500.

After six months, Marcus optimizes the property, increasing income to $4,800 per month. He continues saving and prepares for his next acquisition.

In month nine, Marcus acquires a second property for $520,000. With a similar structure, the property generates $5,000 per month in income with expenses of $3,400, resulting in a cash flow of $1,600.

Now with two properties, Marcus's total monthly cash flow is $3,100.

In month eighteen, Marcus acquires a third property for $550,000. This property generates $5,200 per month in income with expenses of $3,600, resulting in a cash flow of $1,600.

With three properties, Marcus achieves his goal of generating approximately $4,700 per month in cash flow.

By following his execution plan consistently, Marcus is able to move from zero properties to a growing portfolio within two years. Each step builds on the previous one, creating momentum and increasing his financial capacity.

This example demonstrates how execution turns strategy into results. By taking consistent action, making informed decisions, and maintaining focus, Marcus is able to achieve his goals and build a foundation for continued growth.

Final Thoughts

The Mindset, Strategy, and Execution to Build Your Airbnb Empire

You have now completed a journey that very few people ever take the time to fully understand. What began as a simple concept—buying Airbnb properties—has evolved into a complete system for building wealth without relying on traditional income verification. You have learned how to think differently about lending, how to structure deals strategically, how to scale efficiently, and how to manage risk with discipline. But more importantly, you have learned how to take control of your financial future.

The most important realization you should take from this entire book is that the system is not designed to stop you—it is simply designed with rules that most people never learn how to navigate. Traditional lending tells you that your income determines your opportunities. This book has shown you that this is not entirely true. By understanding DSCR loans, asset-based strategies, and creative financing, you have access to a completely different path—one where your ability to structure deals and select strong properties matters more than your tax returns. This shift in perspective is powerful. It means that your future is not limited by how you are paid, what you report on paper, or how a traditional lender evaluates you. Instead, your future is determined by your ability to identify opportunities, analyze deals, and execute consistently. This is a level of control that most people never experience, and it is what makes Airbnb investing with no-income verification such a unique and transformative strategy.

At the same time, it is important to recognize that opportunity comes with responsibility. The strategies outlined in this book provide flexibility, but they also require discipline. You must be intentional in your decisions, conservative in your assumptions, and consistent in your execution. Success in this space is not about taking shortcuts—it is about using the system intelligently and responsibly.

One of the most valuable lessons you should carry forward is the importance of thinking long-term. It is easy to focus on the excitement of acquiring your first property or closing your next deal, but true wealth is built over time. Each property you acquire, each decision you make, and each strategy you implement contributes to a larger picture. By maintaining a long-term perspective, you can make decisions that support sustainable growth rather than short-term gains.

Another key takeaway is the power of consistency. You do not need to move at an extreme pace to succeed. What matters is that you continue moving forward. Each deal, each improvement, and each strategic decision builds momentum. Over time, this momentum compounds, creating results that far exceed what is possible through isolated efforts.

It is also important to understand that challenges are part of the process. Markets will change, deals will fall through, and unexpected situations will arise. These challenges are not signs of failure—they are opportunities to learn and improve. The investors who succeed are those who remain adaptable, resilient, and focused on their goals.

As you move forward, your mindset will play a critical role in your success. Confidence in your strategy, combined with a willingness to take action, is essential. You must trust the process, trust your analysis, and trust your ability to navigate challenges. This confidence is built through experience, and each step you take strengthens it.

Another important aspect of your journey is continuous learning. The real estate and lending landscape is constantly evolving, and staying informed allows you to adapt and refine your strategy. This includes understanding new loan programs, market trends, and operational techniques. By committing to ongoing learning, you ensure that your approach remains effective and relevant. Your network will also play a significant role in your success. Surrounding yourself with knowledgeable professionals and like-minded investors provides valuable insights and support. These relationships can open doors to opportunities, provide guidance, and help you navigate complex situations. Building a strong network is an investment in your long-term success.

As your portfolio grows, you will begin to see the compounding effect of your efforts. Your cash flow will increase, your equity will grow, and your opportunities will expand. This compounding is one of the most powerful forces in real estate investing, and it is what allows you to build significant wealth over time.

At a certain point, your focus may shift from growth to optimization and preservation. This is a natural progression as your portfolio matures. You may begin to prioritize stability, efficiency, and long-term planning. This includes refining your operations, managing risk, and ensuring that your portfolio continues to perform at a high level.

Ultimately, the goal is not just to build wealth—it is to create freedom. Freedom to choose how you spend your time, where you live, and what opportunities you pursue. This freedom is the result of consistent effort, strategic thinking, and disciplined execution. It is not achieved overnight, but it is absolutely achievable for those who commit to the process.

As you reflect on everything you have learned, remember that knowledge alone is not enough. The true value of this book lies in how you apply it. Each concept, each strategy, and each example is a tool that you can use to build your own path. The more you apply these tools, the more confident and capable you will become.

There will always be reasons to wait, to hesitate, or to doubt. But there will also always be opportunities for those who are prepared and willing to act. The difference between where you are today and where you want to be is determined by the actions you take moving forward.

You do not need to have everything figured out before you begin. You simply need to take the first step. From there, each step becomes easier, each decision becomes clearer, and each success builds on the last. This is how momentum is created, and this is how goals are achieved.

The path you are on is not just about investing—it is about transformation. It is about changing how you think, how you approach opportunities, and how you build your future. By embracing this mindset and applying the strategies you have learned, you are positioning yourself for a level of success that goes far beyond financial results. In the end, the most important thing you can do is start. Take action, stay consistent, and continue learning. Trust the process, and allow your efforts to compound over time. The opportunities are there, the tools are in your hands, and the path is clear.

Your Airbnb investing journey does not end here—it begins here.

How to Get a Personalized Airbnb Mortgage Loan Review

If you found this book helpful, you may want to see how these strategies apply to your own financial situation and investment goals. Every investor's profile is unique. Property type, location, projected Airbnb income, credit score, available capital, and lending guidelines all impact what loan programs you may qualify for and how your deal can be structured.

The examples in this book are designed to teach how Airbnb mortgage loans work—but your real options can only be determined by reviewing your specific numbers and investment scenario.

You can request a no-obligation Airbnb mortgage loan consultation here:

Email: info@FinibiMortgage.com

A licensed mortgage professional will review your scenario and explain what Airbnb financing options may be available to you, including DSCR loans, Non-QM programs, and alternative qualification strategies based on your property and financial profile.

No cost. No pressure. No obligation.

Sincerely,

Joseph G. Correa

Licensed Mortgage Loan Originator

Finibi Mortgage Inc.

About the Author

Joseph G. Correa is a licensed mortgage broker and the founder of Finibi Mortgage, a Florida-based brokerage specializing in real estate investment financing, Airbnb and short-term rental loans, and alternative lending strategies for investors, entrepreneurs, and self-employed borrowers. With more than two decades of experience in mortgage lending, underwriting, and financial structuring, Joseph has helped thousands of clients secure funding using intelligent, flexible loan strategies designed for modern real estate investing.

Unlike traditional loan officers who focus only on closing transactions, Joseph's approach is rooted in long-term wealth building. He believes that mortgage financing—especially for Airbnb and investment properties—should be used as a strategic tool to generate cash flow, scale portfolios, and create financial independence. His philosophy centers on using leverage intelligently, allowing investors to grow without relying solely on personal income or traditional lending limitations.

Joseph is widely recognized for his expertise in DSCR loans, Non-QM lending, short-term rental financing, bank statement programs, and creative deal structuring. He specializes in helping investors qualify based on property income rather than personal income, making it possible for beginners, self-employed individuals, and experienced investors to acquire and scale Airbnb portfolios. His ability to simplify complex lending concepts into clear, actionable strategies has empowered countless individuals to enter the real estate market with confidence.

Joseph created *The Airbnb Mortgage Loan Mastery Series* to give investors the same financing knowledge used by banks, private lenders, and institutional real estate operators. His mission is simple: to help people understand how to qualify, structure deals, and scale using modern lending strategies—so they can build profitable Airbnb businesses and long-term wealth.

When he is not structuring deals or writing, Joseph works directly with investors and borrowers across the United States to design customized financing strategies that align with their goals, property types, and growth plans.

The Airbnb Mortgage Loan Mastery Series Roadmap

The Professional Guide to Financing, Scaling, and Profiting from Short-Term Rental Properties

The purpose of *The Airbnb Mortgage Loan Mastery Series* is to give investors the same financing strategies used by banks, lenders, and institutional real estate operators—translated into clear, practical guidance for everyday investors. Each book builds on the last, taking you from foundational knowledge to advanced deal structuring, portfolio scaling, and long-term wealth creation using Airbnb and short-term rental properties.

Book 1 — Airbnb Mortgage Loan Fundamentals
This book gives you the foundation. You will understand how Airbnb mortgage loans work, what makes them different from traditional financing, and how lenders evaluate short-term rental properties. You will learn the core concepts of DSCR, Non-QM loans, and income-based qualification, along with who qualifies and how to structure your first deal. Every book that follows builds on this knowledge and shows you how to apply it to real-world investing.

Book 2 — DSCR Airbnb Mortgage Loans
This book focuses on one of the most powerful tools in Airbnb investing: DSCR loans. You will learn how to qualify using rental income instead of personal income, how DSCR is

calculated using short-term rental data, and how to position your property to meet lender requirements. This book shows you how to break free from traditional income limitations and scale faster.

Book 3 — Airbnb Mortgage Loans for Beginners This book is designed for first-time investors. You will learn how to buy your first Airbnb property using the right loan strategy, how to analyze deals, and how to overcome common obstacles. It provides a clear, step-by-step path from zero experience to your first successful investment.

Book 4 — Airbnb Investment Property Mortgage Loans This book focuses on scaling. You will learn how to finance multiple Airbnb properties, build a portfolio, and optimize cash flow. It introduces strategies for acquiring properties efficiently and managing them as part of a larger system.

Book 5 — Airbnb Mortgage Loans with No Income Verification

This book explores advanced qualification strategies. You will learn how to get approved without tax returns using DSCR, bank statement, and alternative documentation programs. It is designed for self-employed borrowers and investors who want flexibility in how they qualify.

Book 6 — Luxury Airbnb Mortgage Loans

This book focuses on high-end properties. You will learn how to finance luxury Airbnb investments, analyze high average daily rates, and balance risk with return. It introduces jumbo loan strategies and premium market positioning.

Book 7 — Airbnb Mortgage Loans for Vacation Homes

This book explains how to finance second homes and convert them into profitable short-term rentals. You will learn the difference between second home and investment property guidelines, along with hybrid usage strategies and compliance considerations.

Book 8 — Airbnb Mortgage Loan Refinancing & Cash-Out Strategies

This book teaches you how to unlock equity and scale faster. You will learn how to refinance Airbnb properties, execute cash-out strategies, and recycle capital into new investments.

Book 9 — Airbnb Mortgage Loans for Multi-Unit Properties

This book focuses on duplexes, triplexes, and small multifamily properties. You will learn how to finance multiple income streams within one property, analyze mixed rental models, and navigate zoning and compliance.

Book 10 — Advanced Airbnb Mortgage Loan Structuring

This book brings everything together. You will learn how to combine DSCR, asset-based, and creative financing strategies to close complex deals. It is designed for investors who want to operate at a high level and scale without limits.

This series is designed to be followed step by step or used as a reference based on your current stage. Whether you are just starting or already building a portfolio, each book provides the tools, strategies, and insights needed to move forward with clarity and confidence.

The goal is simple: to help you understand how to finance, structure, and scale Airbnb investments so you can build a profitable, long-term real estate business.

Educational & Financial Disclaimer

This book is provided for educational and informational purposes only. The author and publisher are not engaged in rendering legal, tax, accounting, investment, or financial advice. Although Joseph G. Correa is a licensed mortgage loan originator, the information in this book is intended to provide general education about Airbnb mortgage loans, DSCR financing, and short-term rental investment strategies—not personalized financial, legal, or lending advice.

Mortgage programs, underwriting guidelines, interest rates, credit requirements, and short-term rental financing options vary by lender, investor, state, and economic conditions, and may change at any time without notice. The examples, calculations, and scenarios presented in this book are hypothetical and are for illustration purposes only. They do not represent guaranteed results, loan approvals, or actual investment outcomes.

Short-term rental performance, including Airbnb income, occupancy rates, and average daily rates, is influenced by market demand, competition, seasonality, management quality, and local regulations. These factors can vary significantly and are not guaranteed. Before making any financial decisions—including purchasing an Airbnb property, applying for a DSCR or Non-QM loan, refinancing, or using real estate financing for investment purposes—readers should consult with a qualified mortgage professional, financial advisor, tax advisor, or attorney who can evaluate their specific situation.

Risk Disclosure

Real estate investing and short-term rental financing involve risk. Airbnb properties rely on variable income, which can fluctuate due to changes in demand, competition, economic conditions, and local regulations. There is no guarantee that a property will achieve projected income levels or maintain consistent occupancy.

Borrowing to purchase or refinance investment properties increases financial leverage and risk. Failure to make required mortgage payments could result in foreclosure or loss of property. DSCR and Non-QM loans may carry higher interest rates, stricter terms, or prepayment penalties, which can impact long-term profitability.

Additionally, changes in laws or regulations governing short-term rentals may affect your ability to operate a property as an Airbnb. Investors are responsible for ensuring compliance with all local, state, and federal regulations.

This book teaches structured, strategic, and responsible approaches to Airbnb financing and investing, but no strategy is risk-free. Readers are solely responsible for their financial decisions and outcomes. Neither the author nor the publisher makes any warranties, express or implied, regarding the accuracy, completeness, or applicability of the information in this book to any individual situation.

www.ingramcontent.com/pod-product-compliance
Lightning Source LLC
LaVergne TN
LVHW022222200926
848481LV00006B/2077
* 9 7 9 8 2 9 5 8 0 1 2 3 5 *